AF587421

Mysteries of Judaism IV

Over 100 Mistaken Ideas about God and the Bible

Mysteries of Judaism IV

Over 100 Mistaken Ideas about God and the Bible

Israel Drazin

Cover design: Leah Ben Avraham/Noonim Graphics
Typesetting: Raphaël Freeman MISTD, Renana Typesetting

ISBN: 978-965-7023-45-7

1 3 5 7 9 8 6 4 2

Gefen Publishing House Ltd.
6 Hatzvi Street
Jerusalem 94386,
Israel
972-2-538-0247
orders@gefenpublishing.com

Gefen Books
c/o Baker & Taylor Publisher Services
30 Amberwood Parkway
Ashland, Ohio 44805
516-593-1234
orders@gefenpublishing.com

www.gefenpublishing.com

Printed in Israel

Library of Congress Control Number: 2020912204

Dedicated as usual with love to my wife Dina,
my inspiration who makes it possible
for me to write books and articles

Fifty-Four Literary Works by Israel Drazin

MAIMONIDES AND RATIONAL SERIES

Maimonides: Reason above All

Maimonides and the Biblical Prophets

Maimonides: The Extraordinary Mind

A Rational Approach to Judaism and Torah Commentary

Nachmanides: An Unusual Thinker

Mysteries of Judaism I

Mysteries of Judaism II: How the Rabbis and Others Changed Judaism

Mysteries of Judaism III: Common Sense Evaluations of Religious Thoughts

Mysteries of Judaism IV: Over 100 Mistaken Ideas about God and the Bible

Stories that Teach the Truth

UNUSUAL BIBLE INTERPRETATIONS SERIES

Five Books of Moses

Joshua

Judges

Ruth, Esther, and Judith

Jonah and Amos

Hosea

SCHOLARLY TARGUM BOOKS

Targumic Studies

Targum Onkelos to Exodus

Targum Onkelos to Leviticus

Targum Onkelos to Numbers

Targum Onkelos to Deuteronomy

EDITOR OF AND FOREWORD TO:

Living Legends

Abraham – The Father of the Jewish People

EDITOR OF AND FOREWORDS TO NATHAN DRAZIN'S

Legends Worth Living
Abraham – The Father of the Jewish People

FOREWORDS TO MICHAEL LEO SAMUEL'S BOOKS

Maimonides' Hidden Torah Commentary, Genesis, Book One
Maimonides' Hidden Torah Commentary, Genesis, Book Two
Maimonides' Hidden Torah Commentary, Exodus, Book One
Maimonides' Hidden Torah Commentary, Exodus, Book Two
Maimonides' Hidden Torah Commentary, Numbers
Maimonides' Hidden Torah Commentary, Deuteronomy
An Odyssey of Faith
Gentle Jewish Wisdom
Birth and Rebirth Through Genesis 1–11
Birth and Rebirth Through Genesis 12–27

WITH CECIL B. CURREY

For God and Country

WITH STANLEY WAGNER

Understanding the Bible Text: Onkelos on the Torah: Genesis
Understanding the Bible Text: Onkelos on the Torah: Exodus
Understanding the Bible Text: Onkelos on the Torah: Leviticus
Understanding the Bible Text: Onkelos on the Torah: Numbers
Understanding the Bible Text: Onkelos on the Torah: Deuteronomy
Understanding Onkelos
Beyond the Bible Text
Iyunim Betargum (Hebrew)

WITH LEBA LIEDER

Can't Start Passover without the Bread
Sailing on Moti's Ark on Succoth

Just What the Doctor Ordered: Moti's Purim Story

AS DANIEL A. DIAMOND

Around The World in 123 Days

Crisis on Queen Victoria

Rational Religion

NOVEL

She Wanted to Be Jewish

Acknowledgements

Thanks to Darlene Jospe who edited this book and prepared the Index, Table of Contents, and the List of Sources and to Ruth Pepperman who did the final editing.

Contents

Relying on Divine Help

Jewish and Non-Jewish Versions of a Story

Other ideas

Introduction

This is the fourth book in my series called *Mysteries of Judaism* where I give readers an opportunity to understand better the sources and content of sacred Jewish texts, practices, and ideas. Although some of what I write may appear to be non-traditional, I am convinced that what I write is traditional Judaism. I am an observant Orthodox Jew. I look at what the Torah is actually saying, and not what we want it to say. I try to minimize the harm that zealots from various backgrounds use to define and describe Judaism incorrectly, hurting Jews and non-Jews by teaching false ideas, suggesting unnecessary behaviors, and by imposing restrictions on Jews when they are unnecessary.

The books in this series respectfully urge readers to question accepted values and to challenge conventional "reality" in the light of higher ideals, respond to the social requirements of our time, and live a life based on the use of intelligence with a sense of commitment to all human beings. The books also emphasize the teachings of Maimonides, and are designed to be eye-opening while encouraging readers to think.

In the first book of the series, I showed that none of the holy days are observed today as mandated in the Torah, and described why the rabbis had to change the way the days were celebrated. In most instances, the rabbis totally eliminated the biblical concept and developed a new one.

In the second book, I focused mostly on Jewish practices showing the how, why, and value of the changes. The book also illustrated the following:

- Biblical laws fit the needs of the time when constructed.
- The Torah wanted changes to its laws because of new conditions and gave Jewish leaders, including rabbis, the power to alter the Torah laws.

- There are far less than 613 biblical commands. The concept of 613 commands is sermonic.
- Rabbis developed the Oral Torah. God did not reveal the Oral Torah to Moses.
- There were many changes made in the Torah text, including in the wording.
- Changes in Torah laws are for moral considerations to combat non-Jewish practices, and for other reasons.
- Many Jews objected to the changes.
- Jews fast for events on days the events did not occur.
- Ideas like the soul, world to come, and reward and punishment after death are not in the Bible, even though some rabbis insist that they are.

The third book focuses primarily on ideas, and shows that they too changed. Among many things, it includes what the Torah states about life after death, the soul, the world to come, sin, repentance, rational and mystical views on immortality, resurrection, and the age of the universe. The book addresses what if anything we must believe, changes that occurred in our concept of God, multiple violations of Torah laws by biblical persons (even prophets), and why this occurred. It further shows misunderstandings about the Ten Commandments, whether or not the Torah is rational, divine involvement in miracles, prophecies that were not fulfilled, biblical and other ancient Jewish books that were neglected or rejected, and even humor in the Bible. *Mysteries of Judaism III* tries to explain all biblical figures with their faults, and the changing biblical laws and rabbinical customs.

In this fourth volume, I examine over 100 misconceptions about God, the Bible, and other ideas that are central to Judaism. Among the many, I focus on:

- Why is the story of creation placed in the Bible?
- Should one understand the story of creation as an actual event, exactly as described?
- Much in the creation story is obscure and seems to be self-contradictory.
- What can we know about God?
- *Y-H-V-H* and *Elohim* as well as other so-called names of God are not God's names.
- There are multiple questions raised by the Adam and Eve stories, including: Are there two versions about the creation of Eve? Did other people exist before

or during the lifetime of Adam and Eve and their children? Where did Cain, Abel, and Seth get their wives?

- Should Jews accept the concept of original sin? Is it in the Torah?
- Did Adam and Eve really eat a forbidden apple?
- Why does the Torah say it was a talking snake that enticed Eve? Why did the snake do so? Was sex involved? Is the story a parable?
- Understanding the biblical concept of prayer is different from the practice.
- Is it possible that the revelation of the Torah was at Sinai when it describes events that occurred after the Israelites left Sinai?
- Should we accept the finding of Abraham ibn Ezra and Spinoza that Moses could not have composed everything in the Torah given that the primary example as recognized by the Talmud is the tale of Moses's death and burial?
- Should we agree that there are many indications that the biblical figures after the time of Moses until around 620 BCE and maybe later, including prophets and leaders of the people, knew nothing about the Torah and repeatedly violated Torah commands?
- Did Jacob wrestle with an angel and did Balaam speak with his donkey?
- Ishmael and Esau do not appear as bad men in the Torah.
- The Bible does not identify Jerusalem as a holy city or require that it should be the only place for sacrifices. In fact, for 369 years, beginning not very long after the Israelites entered Canaan, Shiloh, where the prophet Samuel lived was the place for sacrifices.
- Could we not call the Shiloh house of God the first temple because it was a humble enclosure?
- Relying on God for help can result in tragedy.
- We do not know how, why, or when most Jewish practices began.
- The practice of reciting the Shema on the deathbed began around 1800 and is based on two legends, both of which are misunderstood.
- The Torah does not mandate saying the Shema twice daily. This is a rabbinical enactment.

The Bible has a style that most people do not know and as a result they fail to understand what the Bible is saying, thus misunderstanding Judaism. Below are some examples.

- The Torah does not tell us everything and leaves much to the reader's imagination.
- Stories often have unrelated stories mixed in regardless of the insertion not having any relationship to the main tale.
- Scripture frequently repeats itself.
- Most numbers in the Torah are arguably exaggerated to highlight the event.
- Repetition often seems to conflict with a prior description in a significant manner.
- Differences in spelling occur frequently, as in the two versions of the Decalogue.
- We can only guess the meaning of many biblical words.
- Christians divided the Torah into chapters, which Jews accepted even though the divisions are not always rational.
- Rabbi Akiva, Rashi, most synagogue sermons, and others insist that the Torah is in divine language, with God saying exactly what God wants said. Rabbi Ishmael, Maimonides, ibn Ezra, and others take the view of the Torah speaking in human language, with repetitions not teaching new lessons, but only repeated for emphasis or a similar reason.
- Some commentators, such as Nachmanides, are convinced that the Torah is composed in a mystical code.
- Scripture frequently, yet briefly describes an event, leaving out details, which it later adds when the story of the event is repeated.
- Both rabbis and scholars differ among themselves whether certain biblical stories or events are actually history or a dream or parable.
- One can better understand Biblical stories by comparing them with other tales in the Bible and outside the Bible.
- The numbers 3, 7, and 10 (being a combination of the first two), occur frequently.

HUGE MISTAKEN BIBLE INTERPRETATIONS

Chapter One
The Creation Stories

> Many interpretations of biblical events improperly teach people to believe something when the event is not what is taught. As a result, people have erroneous ideas about their religion. Sometimes these mistaken notions affect their behavior. The following are examples from the opening chapters of Scripture.

WHY WAS THE STORY OF CREATION INCLUDED IN THE BIBLE?

Many think that the Bible is giving us the true history of the world. Famous commentators such as the Spanish Nachmanides (1194–1270) objected strongly to supposing the Bible has parables similar to *Aesop's Fables,* and insisted that all the stories in the Torah are actual historical events. He also asserted that the stories in Midrashim, despite appearing to be unnatural events, actually happened.

The biblical and talmudic French commentator Rashi (1040–1105) argued in his first Bible commentary that the Torah emphasizes that God created the world and all that is in it, God can do with the world as He sees fit, and God gave the land of Israel to the Jewish people. Jews and non-Jews alike should realize this and not try to thwart God's intention by taking Israel from the Jews.

Many others see the opening chapters as a myth or parable to cause us to think. They read many ethical lessons into the story. Maimonides (1138–1204) even interpreted the story of the Garden of Eden in his *Guide of the Perplexed* 1:2 as a parable. He wrote in his essay called *Chelek* that anyone who thinks that midrashic tales are true events is a fool.

(There is a fancy English word for the methodology used in Midrash, of pulling ideas from the text: "wiredraw." It means to strain unwarrantably. It is based on the practice of workers whose job it was to create wires by forcibly drawing metal through a series of smaller and smaller holes until it was thin enough to be a wire.)

Actually, we have no idea why the Bible starts as it does and can only speculate about the issue.

GOD'S NAMES ARE NOT NAMES

1. The Torah uses many words to describe God, such as *Elohim, Y-H-V-H, Shaddai,* and more. Genesis 1 describes *Elohim* creating or forming the world. *Elohim* simply means God; it is not a name. In chapter 2 on the other hand, from 2:4 the introduction of a new subject uses *Y-H-V-H Elohim,* translated as *Y-H-V-H,* who is God. Perhaps, the Bible is saying in Genesis 1 that God created the world. In Genesis 2, there are details such as how the woman was created, and the Bible identifies the God as *Y-H-V-H.*
2. Other ancient cultures use the noun *El* to denote a god. It is possible that the plural *Elohim* indicates a more powerful God.
3. *Elohim* is also used to denote humans with powers, as in Genesis 6 where *benei Elohim* is translated "sons of God" by many Bible commentators, or influential or exceptionally intelligent men like Abraham ibn Ezra (c. 1089–1167) and others. Similarly, the use of *Elohim* to describe the man who wrestled with Jacob in Genesis 32:29 and 31 could refer to a strong man. Also, the requirement in Exodus 22:8 to bring the litigation to *Elohim* does not mean bring it to God, but to judges, as Rashi and others say.
4. *Y-H-V-H,* like *Elohim,* is not a name, such as Joseph. Both are descriptions. As indicated above, *Elohim* denotes a powerful being. Rabbis and scholars say that *Y-H-V-H* is a word built upon a Hebrew term meaning "being," and indicates that God existed and functioned in the past, does so in the present, and will do so in the future.
5. Words such as *haElohim* in Exodus 3:1, with the prefix *ha* (the), show that *Elohim* is not a name as many suppose.
6. *Y-H-V-H* is frequently written with hyphens like spelling God as G-d. This presumably shows respect for God by not even writing these words completely.
7. This sensitivity and respect also encouraged Jews to replace *Y-H-V-H* when

speaking, but not in the Torah text used in the synagogue, with Adonai, which means Lord. Ever since Greek Jews translated the Bible into Greek around 250 BCE, if not shortly before, when the translators rendered *Y-H-V-H* as *Kurios* (Lord), Jews everywhere stopped using *Y-H-V-H* out of respect to the deity and, like the Greek Jews, substituted "Lord," which is *Adonai* in Hebrew.

8. The rendering of the transliterated Hebrew *Y-H-V-H* into English letters is done today with a *J* instead of a *Y*. The result is Jehovah. The first Hebrew letter is a *yud*. German biblical scholars transliterated many, but not all, Hebrew names that begin with a *yud* with a *J*. Examples of words starting with a *yud* that were transliterated with a *J* include "Jerusalem," "Judea," and "Jew." Words that escaped this *J* transliteration include Israel and Ishmael using the letter *I*. If the transliteration was precise, since the *yud* has a *Y* sound in English, the names should have been Yisrael and Yishmael.
9. Many scholars insist that the use of different names, *Elohim* and *Y-H-V-H*, indicate composition by different authors. This issue aside, many Jews, based on Midrashim, say that Elohim denotes God exercising justice while *Y-H-V-H* indicates God working with mercy. This notion is midrashic, designed to prompt Jews to act properly lest God, *Elohim*, deal with them with justice and punish them. This goal to frighten people to act properly is also why the Bible speaks of God becoming angry.
10. God is all powerful and one. "One" means that God is acting with justice and mercy simultaneously.
11. A careful observation of the usage of *Elohim* and *Y-H-V-H* will reveal that it is not always possible to say that the former refers to justice and the latter to mercy.
12. The name *Y-H-V-H* appears in Scripture frequently in a shortened form *Y-H*. This occurs often in names such as Adoniyah, meaning *Y-H* is my Lord (Adoni). The name Adoniyah, is often spelled as Adonijah because the *yud* is transliterated as a *J*.
13. The Bible depicts God anthropomorphically and anthropopathically, meaning portraying God as having human-like features such as the "arm of God," and describing God showing human emotions. Philosophy teaches us that God has no human physicality and emotions. Most rabbis and philosophers explain that the Bible needed to describe God in a physical manner to help the early Israelites understand what they need to know about God.

WHAT CAN WE KNOW ABOUT GOD?

The Torah makes the study of nature religiously obligatory, a mitzvah, for all people who are capable of studying it. The Bible commands people to love and fear God.[1] Since no one, not even God, can command a person to feel an emotion, to love, or to fear, these basic commands must refer to the obligation to study and learn about God.

In his *Guide of the Perplexed* 1:52 and elsewhere, Maimonides tells us that it is impossible for humans to understand anything about God. He tells us in many places that knowing about God comes through understanding the laws of nature that God created, along with the sciences and philosophy, both of which examine nature. God explained this to Moses saying, "You will see my back (the laws of nature that I created); but my face (my true essence) will not be seen."[2]

GOD CREATED THE WORLD OUT OF NOTHING

Many people are convinced that the Bible clearly states that nothing existed in the world other than God before God created the world. They see this idea of creation ex nihilo meaning creation out of nothing in the wording of the Torah. This is contrary to the view of the rational Greek philosopher Aristotle (384–322 BCE) who said that the world was created from preexisting matter. Maimonides usually accepted the view of Aristotle. In his *Guide of the Perplexed* 1:74, Maimonides states that the biblical account in Genesis 1 can be interpreted either way. Many but not all scholars assert that he accepted the Aristotelian view.

THE WORLD WAS CREATED IN SIX DAYS

Taking the words of Genesis 1 literally, many claim that the world was created in six days, beginning with 1 Tishrei, the date of Rosh Hashanah, and that the world is currently 5,780 years old. This idea is problematical in many ways. Most people are convinced that God is all powerful and did not need to work for six days to create the world. God could have created or formed it during a single day. The

---

1. Maimonides, Moses (Rambam), *Sefer Hamitzvot*, positive commands 3 and 4. See also Deuteronomy 4:39, 6:5, 11:13; Jeremiah 9:23; and 1 Chronicles 28:9.
2. Exodus 33:23. See also Moses Maimonides (Rambam), *The Guide of the Perplexed* (University of Chicago Press, 1974), 3:54.

biblical account is most likely a parable written to emphasize the importance of understanding science. Even if taken literally, there is no indication that the creation of the world occurred in a specific month. In the Talmud there is a rabbi who states it began in the spring while another argues it began in the fall. Rosh Hashanah was not considered the beginning of the year until the Common Era as described in my first *Mysteries of Judaism* book. Also, the calculation of years from creation, called anno mundi, did not begin until around the sixth century CE as described in detail in this same book, which also reveals that it is based on erroneous information.

DURING WHICH MONTH WAS THE WORLD CREATED?

In ancient times, probably since the exile of Judeans into Babylon in 586 BCE when they accepted the Babylonian calendar and the Babylonian names of the months still used in Judaism, the Judeans began to believe that the creation of the world occurred on the first day of Tishrei. The Bible does not state the date of creation. It also states, contrary to the notion that the year begins in Tishrei, that the month later called Nisan is the first month and the month later called Tishrei is the seventh month.[3] In fact, if the six-day events of creation are taken as six periods of time, we can understand the Bible saying that creation was a long process with distinct events happening at different times, so there is no single day of creation.[4] The Talmudic sages knew that we cannot pinpoint a day of creation; they even argued homiletically, as previously stated, about whether the world was created in Nisan or Tishrei.[5]

WHEN WAS THE SUN CREATED?

Genesis 1:1–4 states that God created light on the first day, called the light day and called the darkness night. Verse 5 follows: And there was evening and there was morning, one day.

How is this possible? It is not until the fourth day that the Torah notes the creation of the sun, and we know that day and night, light and darkness, depend

3. Exodus 12:1.
4. Babylonian Talmud, *Ketubot* 57b, *yamim* (days) can mean years.
5. Babylonian Talmud, *Chagigah* 12a, *Rosh Hashanah* 8a, 10b–11a, 27a, *Avoda Zara* 8a.

on the sun. How could the prior verses say that God made light, evening, and morning before the creation of the sun? The rabbis noted the problem. A Midrash offers the view that a brighter and more enjoyable sun than the one created on day four happened on day one but God hid it away for good people to enjoy after they die. There is no hint of this concept in Genesis and there is no mention of an afterlife anywhere in the Torah.

It is possible to say that God created the sun on the first day, as stated in verse 3 and improved it on the fourth day after the creation of vegetation on the third day. The improvement may have been to not only give light as indicated in verses 1–4, but also to support growth and life. There is no hint of this in the text, but is arguably a more reasonable explanation than hiding the sun for the afterlife.

It is also possible since the Torah uses "light" in this section, and not "sun," that it is not referring to the sun, and that the words "light," "day," "evening," and "morning" in these verses are metaphors for "an unidentified creation," made during "an unspecified period of time" "that ended," and "a new period of time began."

WHEN DOES THE DAY BEGIN?

In the Ma Nishtana, the four questions asked during the Seder on Passover, one asks the question, "Why is this night different than all other nights?" There are then four differences mentioned. Many years ago, I heard a respected scholar offering a fifth and startling difference. The night of Passover is different from all other nights. On all other nights when a holiday occurs, just the single holiday is celebrated. The first night of Passover is different because it is the celebration of two holidays.

The Torah states that the holiday of Passover occurs on the fourteenth day of the first month and the Feast of the Unleavened Bread begins on the fifteenth. The Torah also states that the celebration of Passover begins by eating the Pascal lamb sacrificed during the day of the fourteenth until the morning of the fifteenth. The scholar said, since "as all Jews know," the day begins in Judaism at sundown, the Feast of the Unleavened Bread begins during the night when Jews are still celebrating Passover by eating the Pascal lamb.

(This may seem to be confusing. However, as I explain in my book *Mysteries of Judaism I*, the Torah speaks of a holiday called Passover, which is a one-day holiday on the 14th of the first month. This continues the next day, on the fifteenth, with a seven-day holiday called the Feast of the Unleavened Bread. The only celebration of the biblical Passover was the sacrifice and eating of the Pascal sacrifice. When the temple was destroyed in 70 CE and sacrifices ceased, Passover ceased to exist. The rabbis decided to remember Passover by calling the Feast of the Unleavened Bread by the name of Passover. Although, in the siddur [prayer book], the original biblical name continues, Feast of the Unleavened Bread.)

The scholar argued that before 70 CE, when the two holidays existed, and during the night when Feast of the Unleavened Bread began (at nightfall), the Passover celebration of eating the Pascal sacrifice continued, and that night was different than all other nights because two holidays were celebrated at the same time.

He was mistaken, as the sage Rabbi Samuel ben Meir (known as Rashbam, circa 1085–1174) explains in his commentary to Genesis 1:5, the biblical day began in the morning, not in the evening. Scripture states that God did creative acts during the day continuing in the evening and morning, the end of the day. We might add that it was most likely during the Babylonian exile after the destruction of the first temple in 586 BCE that the Israelites accepted the Babylonian practice of starting the day at night. While the beginning of the day changed for other purposes, it did not change the temple service. When the construction of the second temple occurred after the Babylonian exile, the day began in the morning as in the past, with the first sacrifice done in the morning.

Thus, the scholar erred. The biblical holiday Passover began on the morning of the fourteenth and ended the next morning when the fifteenth day of the first month began. The two holidays did not overlap. Rashbam's interpretation explains why the Israelites could eat the pascal lamb during the night until the following morning – because the night was still the fourteenth, still Passover.

THE ORDER OF CREATION

Genesis 1 describes the creation of humans after the creation of animals. Why?

Midrashim explain that God wanted to prepare the world with all that the humans would need before constructing humans. This is a reasonable explanation.

However, some people may argue that the existence of animals before humans is consistent with the theory of evolution.

MORE APPARENT DIFFICULTIES: IS THE ORDER OF CREATION CORRECT?

As is well known, vegetation needs the sun to grow. How, therefore, is vegetation created on day three while the sun did not appear until day four?

WHY WAS THE SNAKE CHOSEN AS THE BEING THAT SEDUCED EVE?

People see snakes today as they were in ancient times as a primal enemy of humans.

It would most likely be a mistake to suppose that the snake symbolized the penis and draw conclusions from it. Midrashim may have had this in mind when they suggested that the snake seduced Eve sexually and Cain was the result of the liaison.

WERE THE TALES OF THE GARDEN OF EDEN ACTUAL EVENTS?

Opinions differ. Rational thinkers such as Maimonides said that the event is a parable, and he gives an explanation in his *Guide of the Perplexed* 1:2. Mystics and literalists such as Nachmanides felt certain that the described events actually happened.

WHY IS THE CREATION OF HUMANS CALLED VERY GOOD?

After every element of creation, except for two, the Bible tells us that God was pleased and said it was "good." God does not say this after dividing creation between heaven and earth on the second day. Similarly, the Bible does not say that God declared "it is good" after the creation of humans in 1:27. Also, in 1:31, after all else and humans were created, God was very pleased and said it was "very good."

Why?

Contrary to what most people think, the Hebrew word *kodesh*, generally translated as "holy," has a practical meaning not a mystical otherworldly one. The word denotes separation. People need to learn to separate themselves from what is harmful and degrading. They need to learn to strive to improve themselves and society. But separating oneself can be good or bad. It has the potential for being good, but is not necessarily so. People who separate from society, and think that they should seclude themselves in a house of prayer, and not spend time with others, not even their spouses, are doing wrong. It is possible that the Torah does not call separation good per se; it depends on how it is used. The Shabbat, for example, is *kodesh,* should a Jew make it so by using the time when they do not work to benefit themselves and others.

Why does the Bible not say that God declared "it is good" after the creation of humans? Like the concept of *kodesh,* humans have the potential of being good, but since created with free will, they can also be bad.

After God prepared the world for humans and made humans, the goal of creation was achieved. It was then that God could say "very good." The world was now ready for humanity.

WHAT IS THE MEANING OF GOOD?

Beside the two exceptions, Scripture tells us that God said that what was done was "good." Most Bible readers feel they know what the Bible is saying. But do they? What is the meaning of "good"? In what way is it "good"? Why is God saying that the creation was good? Is God surprised at the result? Did God think that the result might be bad? Doesn't God have the power to do all God desires? Who is God talking to when the claim is made?

Perhaps God is not talking at all, or even thinking these thoughts. Perhaps it is the Bible telling us that what was created is good, that all was created for humans who, if they use it properly, will live a perfect life and prosper. Perhaps, the chapter is addressing the age-old question of why evil occurs and is saying that the creation was perfect and would have satisfied humans if they had only used it as God had intended it to be used.

THERE ARE QUITE A FEW OBSCURE ITEMS REGARDING CREATION

1. Adam's name means "man" and "human," both appropriate for the first human. Why is Eve not called "woman," the name that Adam gave her in 2:23, when he invented the name *isha,* which is similar to the name *ish,* which means man? Adam said this is an appropriate name since the woman was taken from man. Instead, in Hebrew she is *Chava* (Eve), which means "life," which he called her in 3:20 "because she was the mother of all living." Why did Adam change his wife's name?
2. Are both names demeaning, both suggesting that she is subservient to her husband?

3. Adam called his wife *Chava* before the two had sex. How did he know she would be the mother of all living beings?
4. After the episode with the enticement of the snake, in chapter 4 Adam has sex with Eve and she bears him a son. Eve calls him Cain, which the Bible explains means "to get," because Eve said, "I have gotten a man with the help of the Lord (*Y-H-V-H*)." What kind of help did God give her? Why was she the one who gave the child a name instead of it being a couple's decision?
5. Genesis 1:27 states that God created humans in the "image of God," but does not explain what this means. Maimonides states in his *Guide of the Perplexed* 1:1 that it means that God gave humans intelligence. There is not even a hint of Maimonides's explanation in chapter 1. Should we accept it?

ANSWERS GIVEN BY TRADITIONS

Many traditional answers are given to these and similar questions. The term "tradition" is used frequently in discussions about Jewish values and practices. Maimonides warns us to be skeptical of traditions, no matter what their source, even if quoted from a highly respected rabbi, and no matter how many people insist that the tradition is correct. He writes in his *Commentary on the Aphorisms of Hippocrates* that a person should test the tradition, whether it is a medical treatment taught by the famed physician Hippocrates, or a Jewish value by a learned rabbi, and examine whether it is logical and conforms to science.

Chapter Two
The Torah

Despite the noun Torah being widely used, most people have no idea what Torah means and how it is used in the Bible.

THE MEANING OF TORAH

Torah means teaching. The word is not used in the Bible to describe the Five Books of Moses or Pentateuch, a word meaning "Five (Books)." The Five Books are also called Chumash which in Hebrew means "Five." The Bible uses the word Torah to describe a particular teaching or command under discussion, but not the entire book. It was only in post-biblical times that Torah began as a synonym for Chumash. While many use Torah for the entire Hebrew Bible, others use the acronym Tanakh as the title for the three parts of Scripture: Torah (the Five Books of Moses), Nevi'im (the books of the prophets), and Ketuvim (the other writings).

THE TORAH DOES NOT HAVE CONSISTENT SPELLING

There are many incidences where the Torah uses a given spelling in one verse and a different spelling of the same word in another verse even if the subject is the same. An example is the Decalogue, first found in Exodus 20 and repeated by Moses in Deuteronomy 5 with many of these same words spelled differently.

MANY BIBLICAL WORDS ARE IMPOSSIBLE TO TRANSLATE

People of different religions may be convinced that the Bible contains the words of God and that God is communicating with humans to tell them various things. Therefore, they surmise that since God is most wise, what the Bible states must be clear. Actually, much in the Bible is not clear at all. The following are some examples.

Scripture opens with the statement in verse 1, "In the beginning, God created the heaven and the earth." The Hebrew word *shamayim* (heaven) is plural. We do not know why. The plural form led many to think that there are increasing levels of heaven, and God sits in the seventh heaven. Maimonides wrote in his essay called *Chelek* that heaven does not exist and people are not going there when they die. Science also confirms that there is no place called heaven. So, what is the Bible saying?

Verse 2 states, "The earth was unformed and void, and darkness was upon the face of the deep, and the spirit of God hovered over the face of the water." The Hebrew words *tohu vavohu,* translated here "unformed and void," are obscure; we really have no idea how to translate them. We also do not know what the Bible is saying. Is it saying that the earth existed before creation and was in some kind of unformed state?

Is the verse saying that water existed before creation in verses 9 and 10 when it states that God said on the third day, "Let the waters under the heaven be gathered unto one place, and let dry land appear. And it was so. And God called the dry land earth." Do these verses concerning the creation of earth on the third day conflict with verse 1, which states that God created earth in the beginning? The Bible commentator Rashi agrees that there is a conflict and states that verse 1 is not saying that the creation of heaven and earth happened on day one. The opening verse should be translated, "In the beginning *when* (meaning, during the time when later) God created the heaven and the earth."

Other unclear words in verse 2 are "deep" and "spirit of God." What is meant by these?

Does the obscurity of some biblical words suggest that the Torah is not as good as we thought it was? No. Just the opposite. These obscurities make us think.

HOW WAS LIFE DIFFERENT IN BIBLICAL DAYS?

Not only are some words difficult to understand, we need to decide how life today is different from biblical days. In his preface to *Caesar and Cleopatra,*[1] the

1. George Bernard Shaw, *Caesar and Cleopatra* (Penguin Classics, 2006).

Nobel Prize laureate, author George Bernard Shaw wrote that he could describe the emotions and acts of Caesar and Cleopatra because people of the past are the same as people today.

In Judaism, there are two views. Many ultra-Orthodox Jews are convinced that there is a decline in intelligence over the generations. If we are humans, the ancients were angels. If the ancients were humans, we are like animals.

Rational thinkers like Maimonides felt the opposite. People have been improving. The ancients thought they needed to offer sacrifices and needed slaves to endure. Modern thinkers realize this is not true.

Menachem Kellner, in his important and very clearly written book about Maimonides on the *Decline of the Generations and the Nature of Rabbinic Authority*,[2] explains that Maimonides rejected the notion of the decline of the generations out of hand. Maimonides was convinced that the ancient rabbis were ordinary human beings possessing no supernatural intellectual powers and they did not base their decisions on divine revelation. Maimonides recognized the authority of the earlier rabbis and accepted their decisions only because each of their rulings "derives from the role they played in Jewish history." Maimonides was thus expressing the belief that the rabbinic decisions were not correct per se, but since the majority of Jews had decided to accept the early rabbis' halakhic decisions, they became authoritative.

There are other changes beside intelligence that need to be considered when we read the Torah. For example: When the Torah speaks about money it always places silver before gold, in Hebrew, *kesef v'zahav*. In ancient times was silver more precious than gold?

JEWS DID NOT DIVIDE THE TANAKH INTO CHAPTERS

Christians came up with the idea of dividing the Bible into chapters so that it would be easy to refer to various parts. For example, the Decalogue is in Exodus 20 and Deuteronomy 5. Jews accepted many of the divisions, but not all. For instance, the Christian Bible has four chapters for the book Malachi, but the Hebrew bible has only three. Many of the chapter divisions, although accepted by Jews, do not

2. Menachem Kellner, *Maimonides on the "Decline of the Generations" and the Nature of Rabbinic Authority* (NY: SUNY Press, 1996).

make sense. An example is the report of the seventh day of creation in Genesis 2:1–3, which should be in chapter 1.

WHAT DOES THE PENTATEUCH WANT TO TEACH PEOPLE?

The Tanakh does not teach beliefs or that people should have faith. It teaches proper behavior.

Contrary to the view of many, the Torah and its halakhot (laws) are not the end goal, but only the means. The Torah is certainly sacred, but one must understand and use it properly. Maimonides devoted chapters 30 through 50 of his third book of the *Guide of the Perplexed* to explaining the 613 biblical commands. He starts his explanation by telling us that the "principal object of the law is to remove this doctrine [idolatry], and to destroy its traces." He explains that God wanted to remove "error from our minds, and protect our bodies from trouble; and therefore, desired us to discontinue the practice of these useless actions." Thus, the first purpose of the law is to renounce and relinquish useless ideas and to prepare ourselves to act properly.

Maimonides writes in chapter 31 that "each and every one of the 613 biblical precepts serves to (1) inculcate some truth, to remove some erroneous idea, (2) to establish proper relations in society so as to diminish evil, and (3) to train [the individual in] good manners and to warn [the person] against bad habits." Thus, Maimonides explains, the biblical laws are "only the means that He employed for His primary [three-fold] objective."

It therefore seems to follow that the pious individual who spends his time studying Torah without involving himself in proper behavior, is mistakenly treating the study of Torah as the goal, while, according to Maimonides, it is only the means to the goal. Such a person is like the carpenter who spends all his time reading the carpentry manual and does not repair the broken table.

DOES EVERY BIBLICAL COMMAND HELP EVERY INDIVIDUAL?

While many would like to insist that laws, especially divine laws, are applicable and beneficial to all people, Maimonides recognizes that this is impossible. In chapter 34, he writes that the law "does not take into consideration exceptional circumstances. . . . It ignores the injury that it could cause a single person. . . . [It is like] nature whose various forces yield general benefits, but cause injury to others.... We should therefore not be surprised when we discover that the object of the law was not fully realized in every person.... It is impossible to be otherwise."

Jewish law takes cognizance of the fact that the law can improperly hurt an individual by several means. When the Israelites had a king, he was allowed to use his judgment and ignore the law in deciding cases. Jewish judges are encouraged when appropriate to decide a case based on "mercy" rather than on the strict rule of the law. There is also a concept of *lifnim meshurat hadin,* which simply stated encourages people in certain circumstances to go beyond the letter of the law.

SHOULD BIBLICAL LAWS CONSIDER CHANGE WHEN CONDITIONS CHANGE?

Maimonides also recognizes that people and conditions change and this affects the laws. In chapter 32, he points out that animals and humans develop slowly from infancy into maturity. It is the same with societies, and the Jews were no exception. "It is impossible to go suddenly from one extreme to another. Therefore, human nature makes it impossible for a person to suddenly discontinue the things to which he was accustomed." Thus, since the Israelites were accustomed to offering sacrifices, "God allowed these kinds of services to continue." The prophets, he wrote, spoke against the sacrifices, because the people misused them in their days.

While recognizing that some laws were instituted (or rather allowed) because of the conditions of the time, and implying that the laws will need to be changed when conditions change, Maimonides does not openly advocate for or against change, and he presents no program for it.

HOW SHOULD LAWS CHANGE?

This brings us to a serious point, which is the difficulty people have in accepting change. It's a complex problem that has not been resolved as it involves not only the psychological difficulty of handling change, but other matters such as different philosophies of law, the interrelationship between what one wants to change and what one wants to leave as is, and the affect that one has on the other. The three major movements of Judaism approach the problem of change differently.

Many of the adherents of Orthodoxy accept the need for change, but focus on the problems. Changes made along the way need a gradual acceptance. Conversely, many Reform Jews concentrate on the needs of current society and suggest quick adjustments. The Conservative movement generally takes an intermediate approach.

DOES THE TORAH TELL US TO PRAY?

The rabbis disagree whether the Torah mandates that Jews must pray. Relying on *Midrash Sifrei*, Maimonides lists praying as two of the 613 commandments, as the fifth and tenth positive commands.

1. The Torah speaks about "serving" God in several places in the Torah, such as Exodus 23:25 and Deuteronomy 6:13, and despite there being no indication in the passage that "serve" means prayer, the Midrash states this is what it means. Others, more realistically, say that "serve" means obey the divine commands.
2. (I believe that Maimonides may not have personally believed that God needed prayers, but he counted the commands totaling 613 that the rabbis felt were included either explicitly or implicitly in the Torah. I am also convinced that Maimonides did not think that God helps people in need, as stated in the next section.)
3. Maimonides also included among the 613 commandments that Jews are obligated to recite the Shema twice daily because the rabbis in the Babylonian Talmud, *Berakhot* 21a saw this command in Deuteronomy 6:7.

SOME MORE THOUGHTS ON PRAYER

Probably every person today has his and her individual approach to prayer. The English word "prayer" derived from the Greek denotes a petition and entreaty, a request for something. It supposes that the deity is capable and willing to grant the petitioner's request.

The Hebrew word for prayer rejects the idea that a person is addressing God. The word *hitpaleil* means "judging oneself," and suggests that the individual is using the traditional formula words as a prompt for self-evaluation, a time to think about the past and future, and resolve to take corrective actions.

Mystics spurn both views. They see prayer as a period of communion, a sense of joining with God when the individual finds contentment, and being part of the whole. Rationalists say it is impossible to join with God.

Others feel an obligation to pray because prayers may possibly fulfill a human requirement to praise God, and to mention many divine attributes such as being merciful, just, and compassionate. Rationalists reject this idea and say that it is hard to believe that God has an inferiority complex and needs praise.

Still others see prayer as a way of saying "thank you." There are also other ideas about prayer.

Most philosophers reject them all including prayer being a period to judge oneself. They write that God has no need for prayers and does not hear them. The world functions according to the laws of nature and will not change no matter how passionately one requests that God alter nature. God is transcendent and it is impossible to join with God. Extolling God for having certain attributes is actually insulting, as one cannot understand God. Whatever we can say about God falls far short of what God is. True, it is good to have a period of self-reflection, but there are far better ways of doing this than a formal service using formulistic words. People, they say, should spend their time bettering themselves and society.

These ideas relate to current prayers, but "prayers" as they are used today are totally unlike many but perhaps not all prayers in the Hebrew Bible. In fact, the Hebrew Bible concept of prayers and the post-biblical versions are so distinct, that one can safely say that prayers did not exist in the Hebrew Bible. Why?

The Hebrew Bible pictures God as being ever present, a being that one can talk to, just as God had a conversation with Adam and Eve while they were in the Garden of Eden. Thus, when Moses asked God to do something such as healing his sister Miriam, this was not what we understand as prayer today; Moses was simply requesting God, with Whom he had frequent conversations and Who he knew was very powerful, to heal his sick sister. Biblical people speak, cry, shout, ask God, as one "person" talks to another, but they do not "pray" to God.

The Israelites offered sacrifices, but there is no evidence in any scriptural book that prayer accompanied sacrifices. True, the Bible has psalms, but there is nothing in the Bible that indicates their usage as prayers.

Moshe Greenberg, who died in May 2010, was a distinguished professor of Bible. He discusses the ancient prayers in his *Biblical Prose Prayer*.[3]

Greenberg shows that these conversations are not formal statements, espe-

---

3. Moshe Greenberg, *Biblical Prose and Prayer*, The Taubman Lectures in Jewish Studies, Book 6, Reprint (Eugene, OR: Wipf and Stock Publishers, 2008).

cially composed words, phrases, and sentences written by priests or poets, but normal everyday human requests that focus on the needs of the specific person at the specific time. They are simple, to the point, and anyone can recite them, even non-priests at any time and at any place. Thus, Moses's prayer on behalf of his sick sister, "O God, please, heal her please," was a simple request that Moses made to God, who was present. It was as mundane as a man needing money for a pay phone, turning to his friend, who is standing near him, and saying, "Frank, please, lend me a quarter."

Greenberg recognizes that some prayers start with "confessions," admissions by the petitioner that he did something wrong. The one who prays hopes that he can now reestablish a good relationship, and that God will grant his request. Greenberg stresses that this not only occurs in addresses to God, but from person to person as well. "I'm sorry that I didn't call you last week, Frank, but could you lend me the quarter please."

In summary, it should be clear that the current understandings that prayers are an entreaty, a self-analysis, a time of communion, or a need to praise God, did not exist in the early biblical period. Biblical personal encounters with God were simply conversations, formed with the same informality as human conversations. Prayers as we understand them today developed later when people developed a feeling that God was not present, but transcendental, loftier, more inaccessible. This was when the people felt that they needed to address such a Deity with elevated formal language, words composed by experts, priests, and poets.

DID GOD DICTATE THE TORAH TO MOSES?

Many Jews, especially many Orthodox Jews, believe that God dictated the Torah to Moses. This was the view of Rabbi Akiva and others. Some say that the Israelites received the Torah at Sinai. This cannot be true since the Torah records episodes occurring to the Israelites after Sinai and the people did not return to Sinai to get the Torah. Many people believe that Moses wrote the entire Torah. But others, such as Abraham ibn Ezra point to Deuteronomy 34:6: "He [God] buried him [Moses] in the valley of Moab, over against Beth-peor; but no one knows where his sepulcher is unto this day." Additionally, the phrase "unto this day" seems to imply composition of this verse a long time after Moses's death. Thus, Moses who was dead could not have written this verse.

The Talmud has a dispute: one sage contended that Joshua wrote the last chapter of the Pentateuch or most of it. The other insisted that Moses wrote even 34:6 at the dictation of God with tears in his eyes. Abraham ibn Ezra uses this biblical section to teach what he calls the Secret of the Twelve. The secret is that Moses could not have written a half a dozen verses in the Pentateuch. Baruch Spinoza lists more than a half dozen.[4]

There are also other opinions and people differ on this subject.

DID THE TORAH EXIST DURING THE DAYS OF MOSES?

While most observant Jews believe that the Torah existed during the days of Moses, some scholars claim that it did not, and only part of it, a version of Deuteronomy, was found during the days of King Josiah in 622 BCE.

1. They point out that the Five Books of Moses, the Pentateuch, makes no mention of a book or books of the Torah. The word "Torah" in the Pentateuch means "teaching" and always refers to a particular command.
2. The Pentateuch does not say that God dictated the Torah to Moses.
3. It does not say that Moses wrote the Torah.
4. While the Decalogue was considered an important item and was placed in the Ark, no Torah was placed in it (Exodus 23:21).
5. Most astonishing is the view of some commentators that the book reveals that the Israelites knew nothing about Moses's Torah. There is, for example, no indication in Joshua, or other biblical books prior to the time of King Josiah – who died in 609 BCE, more than five centuries after Joshua – that the Israelites observed biblical commandments such as the Sabbath.
6. No biblical leader or prophet of the early period who constantly criticized the nation for idol worship reprimanded them for not observing Torah commands. It is reasonable to think that a nation that abandoned serving God and was worshipping idols stopped observing at least some of the divine commands, but the leaders did not mention this.
7. There are conflicts with certain statements in the Pentateuch. A glaring apparent inconsistency is that according to Deuteronomy 20:10–14 the Israelites

4. For more details see, Israel Drazin, *A Rational Approach to Judaism and Torah Commentary* (Urim Publications, 2006).

must try to establish peace with Canaanite nations prior to engaging in a battle with them, but Joshua never did that, nor does the book suggest he even considered it.

8. More remarkably, Deuteronomy 20:10 mandates that the Israelites must expel every Canaanite from the land lest they seduce the Israelites to worship idols. But the Israelites allowed Canaanites to remain in the country and took tribute from them, until the Canaanites grew strong and enticed many to worship idols. The Israelites not only failed to obey this Torah divine command, but there is no indication that they considered it – suggesting that they did not know about it.
9. Exodus 28:30, Leviticus 8:8, Numbers 27:21, and Deuteronomy 33:8 speak about an Urim that the high priest wore to communicate with God to secure divine guidance. This Urim is not in any of the early post-Pentateuch biblical books. Israelite leaders did not utilize it to make decisions. (The Urim is in Ezra 2:63 and Nehemiah 7:65 as a hope for the future, but it was not in use at the time and these books were composed after the first temple period when all agree that the Torah existed. The Urim is mentioned in 1 Samuel 28:6 where it states that God did not answer King Saul by any means, not by dreams, the Urim, or prophets. It does not speak of the use of the Urim and it may be a late interpolation.)
10. Moses's Torah states the need to establish cities of refuge, but there is no evidence that such cities actually existed in biblical books or other literature. True, they are mentioned in a chapter in Joshua, but since there is no indication that they were in use, and in view of other evidence,[5] scholars feel that this chapter was composed centuries after the time of Joshua,[6] and it reflects an ideal situation that was never realized.[7]
11. Another seeming proof that the early Israelites did not know about Moses's

5. Discussed and explained in Menachem Haran, ed. *Olam Hatanakh* (Jerusalem: Gefen Publishing House, 2002).

6. Some of the cities assigned as cities of refuge and as Levite towns were not conquered by Israel until the time of King David, suggesting a late composition of the book Joshua (*Olam Hatanakh*).

7. The book's reference to Moses does not suggest that his Torah was known during the early period of Joshua since these scholars argue that the Torah was not composed until centuries after Joshua's death.

Torah is in Deuteronomy 17:14–20. It states that when Israelites settle in Canaan and desire to appoint a king, they may do so,[8] but the king is restricted in certain ways. Yet 1 Samuel 8 and 12 describe Israelites requesting the prophet Samuel to appoint a king for them, and he scolds them and says he is opposed to a monarchy. Why didn't the people respond by reminding him of Deuteronomy 17? Is it possible that neither they nor he knew anything about Deuteronomy 17?

12. The *Mishkan*, a core element of the religious practices according to the Five Books of Moses,[9] is not mentioned in post-Pentateuch books, and is another indicator that the generations between Moses and the time of King Josiah did not know about the Torah, and therefore did not observe it.
13. Deuteronomy 12:10–14 states that when the Israelites settled in Canaan, they may not "offer your burnt-offerings in every place that you see, but only in the place that the Lord will choose in one of your tribes,"[10] and this place was Shiloh. Yet we know that the Israelites built altars like the ones mentioned in Judges 18, and the two altars established when Israel broke away from Judah during the early reign of King Solomon's son. The fact that none of the biblical books mention anyone criticizing the building of altars as a violation of Deuteronomy 12 until the book of Kings,[11] which was composed after the time of King Josiah, seems to add another possible indication that the pre–King Josiah Israelites knew nothing about Moses's Torah.
14. In Joshua 22, the Israelites assert that they still suffer from the crime of Peor.[12] This claim seems to be another possible indication that the post-Moses Israelites did not know of the existence of the Torah until the time of King Josiah. They could not claim that they were impure from the crime of Peor,[13] when

---

8. Moses Maimonides (Rambam), *Mishneh Torah, Hilkhot Melakhim* 1:1, understood that the Torah obligated the Israelites to appoint a king when they entered Canaan.
9. This is discussed in detail in my book *Unusual Bible Interpretations: Joshua* (Jerusalem: Gefen Publishing House, 2014), chapter 32 (Joshua 22).
10. See also *Midrash Sifrei* on this verse and Babylonian Talmud, *Zevachim* 118b, which discuss this prohibition. Rashi understood that the western tribes were bothered because of the violation of Deuteronomy 12.
11. See, for example, 1 Kings 13.
12. Numbers 25.
13. Joshua 22:17.

Numbers 25:13 and Deuteronomy 4:3–4 state that the Israelites who survived the plague that followed the crime were absolved of all guilt.[14]

15. Additionally, some post-Moses practices are significantly different from those mentioned in Moses's Torah such as the levirate marriage of Ruth. One might ask why they changed the Torah practice?[15]
16. I studied the actions of all of the biblical leaders in my books on the Bible and found that they had no knowledge of the Torah until the time of King Josiah. One example is the book of Samuel. I found 266 verses that deal with the prophet and thirty of them, over 10 percent, show that the author of this biblical book had no knowledge of Moses's Torah. Samuel, like other leaders violated the Torah commands, and the authors of these pre-Josiah books do not criticize their behaviors.

SUMMARY

The ancient rabbis recognized these apparent problems and they provided answers that showed observance of the Torah after the time of Moses. I gave some of the answers offered by the rabbis in my books on these parts of the Tanakh.

---

14. It could be argued that they knew of these statements, but were saying that despite what God said they still felt guilty.

15. I explained in my books such as *Mysteries of Judaism 1* (Jerusalem: Gefen Publishing House, 2014) that the Torah allowed, even encouraged, the development of laws to fit changed circumstances, and the rabbis did make changes. These included the abolition of slavery and sacrifices.

Chapter Three
Adam and Eve

Several biblical stories about Adam and Eve raise many questions that most people prefer to overlook, or to give a glib answer to the problems. The following are a few of the difficulties.

THERE WERE TWO CREATIONS OF ADAM

Genesis 1:27 states, "God created man in his image, in the image of God He created him; male and female He created them." This verse seems to be saying that God created the man and the woman at the same time. Yet Genesis 2:20–22 states that after creating Adam and seeing he had no "help meet," God created the woman out of his side (many translations say "rib") which is clearly different than chapter 1. This led many scholars to claim that chapter 1 was from one author and chapter 2 from another. It has also caused some people to accept the fantasy contained in some Midrashim and in the discussion by the humorist Aristophanes in *The Symposium,* the philosophical book by Plato (c. 428–348 BCE), that humans were originally created with a man being connected with a woman as a single being, which was later separated.

However, there is no difficulty when one recognizes the often-repeated biblical style of the Bible making a broad statement and only later giving the details. Chapter 1 states that God created a man and woman, and chapter 2 explains this creation.

WERE ADAM, EVE, AND FAMILY THE ONLY PEOPLE ON EARTH?

Although there is no proof that other humans existed, it is reasonable to suppose that Adam, Eve, and their three sons were not the only humans during the early postcreation years.[1] One of the biblical writing methods is not to reveal everything, but to leave it to the reader to figure it out.

We can investigate the issue by looking at some possible indicators.

1. When the Bible has a list of people it generally does not list everyone. It often excludes females. In Genesis 5, for example, where the ten generations from Adam to Noah are listed, only a single person from each generation is named. Similarly, in chapter 10, where the Bible lists the descendants of Noah, it does not include the females. Listing only Adam, Eve and their three sons without mentioning the existence of other people at the time is consistent with the general biblical style and should not dispose us to think that they did not exist.
2. Cain, Abel, and Seth's wives are not mentioned. When was their creation? A Midrash suggests that a female twin was born with each son. This would mean that they bedded their twin sisters. This explanation is not in the text. It is contrary to the moral stand of the later Torah, which forbids a man marrying a sister. It is arguably more reasonable to suppose that other people existed at the time.
3. Similarly, the Torah states that Adam and Eve did not have their son Seth until Adam was 130 years old. What happened during the 130 years? Is it possible that he abstained from sex during all these years? It is more likely, that he had many children, male and female, during this time, but true to its style, the Bible does not mention everything that occurs. Seth is mentioned since he was an ancestor of Abraham.
4. In Genesis 4:14, Cain tells God that he is afraid that "whoever finds me will kill me" (perhaps in revenge for killing Abel). Who does he fear? If we accept the idea that only Cain, his parents, and perhaps his and Abel's wife, were alive, should we interpret "whoever" to refer to them? If he meant his relatives, why doesn't he say so? Is it reasonable that he is afraid of his relatives? Wouldn't it be more reasonable to say he feared the non-relatives who also existed at that time?
5. In response to Cain's fear, God placed a sign for Cain. If only the family existed, why would a sign be necessary and why does the Bible say that God placed

1. Adam and Eve bore Cain and Abel soon after creation. They had Seth when Adam was 130 years old.

the sign "lest any finding him should slay him"? The words "any finding him" does not seem to fit the small family.

6. Cain goes out in 4:16 and "dwelt in the land of Nod." If no other people lived at the time, why is there a land of Nod?
7. In verse 7, Cain builds a city and names it after his son. If only he, his wife, son, and possibly Abel's widow lived at the time, and he left his parents, why build a city?
8. Chapter 4 states that Abel kept sheep and Cain was a tiller of the ground. If only the small family existed, why would the brothers need to engage in these vocations? Surely, for example, if Adam and his small family were meat eaters, they could easily find an animal. There was no need for Abel to raise sheep unless he was doing so for other people.
9. True, 1:26 has God state "Let us make man in our image, after our likeness" and in 2:7 the Torah states, "Then the Lord God formed man of the dust of the ground." Usually this means that "man" in these verses denotes a single individual. However, "man" could mean "humans" in the plural. Also, there is no explicit statement in Scripture that there were no other humans that God created. Yes, later in chapter 5, the Bible only gives us the genealogy of Adam and Eve and mentions no other humans existing. But, as previously noted, this genealogy is not complete. Also, it focuses on the descendants of Adam and Eve simply because these are the people who are important to the story as they are the ancestors of Abraham.

These ideas seem to suggest the possibility of the existence of more than the small Adam and Eve family.

WERE THE PRE-NOAHIDE PEOPLE VEGETARIANS?

Many Bible commentators say they were. God told them they could eat the fruits of trees in 1:29 and 2:16, perhaps suggesting that this would be their total diet, and God does not mention eating meat until after the Flood in 9:3–4.

Why did God allow Noah and his family to kill animals for food? Midrashim noted that 6:9 states that Noah was "in his generation a man righteous and whole-hearted and walked with God." Noting the words "in his generation," the Midrashim comment that Noah could be considered a good man only in comparison to his generation, which was corrupt, but if he lived in Abraham's generation, he would not be called righteous. Additionally, soon after the Flood, in 9:20–27, Noah planted a vineyard and became drunk and his son Ham abused him. It is possible that just as God allowed sacrifices (discussed in the next section) because humans felt the need to show God love with sacrifices, God "allowed" the consumption of animal flesh because Noah felt a need to eat it. As George Bernard Shaw said, "I choose not to make a graveyard of my body for the rotting corpses of dead animals."

NAMING ANIMALS

Genesis 2:18 states that God recognized that Adam needed a "help meet." Verses 19–20, describe God bringing animals to Adam to name them. Verse 20 ends by saying "but for Adam there was not found a help meet for him." Verse 21 follows with the story of the creation of Eve.

1. Why is the search for a help meet for Adam, Hebrew *eizer kenegdo,* interrupted by the tale of God bringing animals to Adam for him to name them?
2. What is the meaning of *eizer kenegdo*? What is a "help meet"?
3. Why did God want Adam to name the animals?
4. What kind of names did Adam give to the animals?
5. Why doesn't the Bible tell us why God brought the animals to Adam and what he called them?
6. Should we understand that God thought that animals would satisfy Adam's needs?
7. How would they do so?
8. Shouldn't the all-wise God know that animals would not satisfy Adam's needs?
9. What were Adam's needs? Were they sexual, companionship, or something else?
10. Why did the snake approach the newly created woman and not the man?

THE FALL OF MAN

Christianity interprets Eve and Adam's disregard of the divine command not to eat of a certain tree as "the fall of man," and the "original sin." They meant that these two individuals performed such a terrible act that it affected all their future offspring and people could only be saved from Adam and Eve's sin by believing in Jesus who came to earth to save humanity from this catastrophe. Significantly, the Bible does not even hint of this idea and the early Christians knew nothing about it until Augustine (354–430) invented the notion.

CLOTHING

What is the significance of Adam and Eve's feeling they were naked and needed clothing after they ate the fruit of the forbidden tree? Are those who interpret the feeling of nakedness as an awakening of the sexual drive correct? What does sex have to do with eating a fruit?

WHO WAS THE BETTER PERSON, CAIN OR ABEL?

It is possible to see the tale of Cain and Abel in a different light.

1. Cain became a farmer. This is very difficult work. Abel opted to be a shepherd, arguably a lazy activity. Why does the Bible seem to prefer Abel?
2. Why did Abel think that God wanted him to murder (sacrifice) a living being that God created?
3. How did the two brothers know which sacrifice God preferred?
4. Is God guilty as an accomplice to the murder because He should not have shown preference?
5. Shouldn't the all-knowing God know what would happen when God preferred one sacrifice over another?
6. Should Cain be punished for murder when he was never told it was wrong?
7. Is it possible that he just meant to hurt his brother and had no concept that people die?
8. Why are we not told how the parents of the two boys viewed the episode?
9. Why didn't Adam and Eve intervene to reconcile Cain to Abel?
10. Why didn't Abel try to explain the situation to Cain and make him feel better?

DO THE SACRIFICES OF ABEL AND NOAH DISPROVE MAIMONIDES'S VIEW ABOUT SACRIFICES?

In his *Guide of the Perplexed* 3:32, Maimonides states that God neither needs nor wants sacrifices, but only "allowed" them because ancient people needed to show God love in this way. Maimonides supported his view with the opinion of some ancient prophets. In essence, he said, God had to deal with the mind-set and emotions of people. (This also explains, as I noted in prior *Mysteries of Judaism* books, why the Torah allowed such things as slavery.)

Does the Torah stating that God accepted Abel and Noah's sacrifices prove that Maimonides was wrong? We can give at least two replies. First, all it shows is that humans felt the need for sacrifices from the earliest period of creation. Second, it is possible to see that the Bible is hinting that sacrifices lead to bad consequences: Cain killed Abel because of the sacrifices – perhaps because of jealousy, God accepted Abel's sacrifice and not his. Noah seemingly made a party in celebration of his sacrifice, became drunk, and was abused.

WHY ARE ALL OR VIRTUALLY ALL BIBLICAL PEOPLE DEPICTED DOING WRONGS?

Virtually all biblical people do wrongs, including the first and second generations after creation. People believe that the purpose of the Hebrew Bible is to depict people with behaviors that we should copy, religious, moral, and intelligent people. This is a mistake. Scripture takes a better approach. It describes the behaviors of normal human beings, which includes the first humans and the patriarchs, with their proper and improper behaviors, and with consequences that result from wrong acts. They are humans like us. They also make mistakes. The Torah describes them as they are, and the purpose of these descriptions is for us to learn to avoid their mistakes.

THE TALE OF THE TOWER OF BABEL

Another example where the Torah makes a statement and later follows it with details of how it came about is in Genesis 10 and 11. In the former chapter, the Bible tells us that humanity divided into many nations speaking different languages. Chapter 11, seems to conflict with this. It begins by stating; "Now the entire earth spoke one language and one speech." It goes on to describe the then-existing people as being one nation divided into many nations speaking many languages only after God punished the people for building a tower to ascend to heaven. Understanding the biblical style, one realizes that chapter 11 describes how the situation in chapter 10 came about, just as Genesis 2 explains the creation of Eve.

THE NAME BABEL

The Bible frequently relates the origin of names in a poetic and sermonic, but not linguistic manner even though it claims that it is giving a linguistic reason. The name of Babylon was not because God had mixed up the languages of the people at the tower of Babel. The root of the Hebrew word for "mix" is *b-l-l,* while the root of "Babylon" is *b-b-l.* These words are not related. It is possible that Babylon meant the word for lord (god), Baal.

ADAM AND EVE DID NOT EAT AN APPLE FROM THE FORBIDDEN TREE

The notion that the fruit from the forbidden "tree of good and evil" was an apple is of unknown origin. The Bible does not say this and the fruit could have been other foods including the tomato and the etrog. It is more reasonable to say that the tree in the Bible was a parable, and not specifically an apple tree but a "tree of good and evil." This type of tree does not exist today, nor does its fruit exist today, and if one needs to name the fruit, it would be "fruit of the tree of good and evil."

ADAM LIED TO HIS WIFE RESULTING IN A CATASTROPHE

Genesis 2:16–17 states that before Eve was created, "The Lord God commanded the man, saying: 'You may eat of every tree of the Garden; except the tree of the knowledge of good and evil, you may not eat of it.'" In 3:3, Eve tells the serpent who was seducing her, "God said: 'You may not eat of it, nor touch it.'"

The widely-known interpretation of Eve's idea that God commanded both a prohibition of eating the tree's fruit as well as not touching it is that God did not forbid touching the tree. Adam was the one who added this prohibition. He wanted to assure that Eve not eat the fruit, so he added the prohibition not to touch the tree; he was convinced that if Eve thought she could not even touch the tree, she would not give way to a temptation to eat the fruit.

There are many problems with this interpretation. What made Adam think Eve needed this extra caution? God did not think that Adam needed it. It is sexist. It assumes that Adam felt that Eve lacked self-control, and he needed to lie to her to protect her. The very first relationship between the pair was a lie.

Additionally, the interpretation is based on an unfamiliarity with biblical narratives. The biblical style of telling stories is that when an event is discussed later in the text, the Bible gives some information in the first telling, and adds to that information when the event is later mentioned. Actually, God prohibited the eating and touching. We will discuss this biblical writing style in a later chapter.

The idea in the tale that Adam added to the divine command is based on the rabbinical invention, mentioned in *Ethics of the Fathers* 1:1, "make a fence around [or for] the Torah." As Rabbi Joseph B. Soloveitchik explains in his *Days of Deliverance* and in *The Koren Mesorat Harav Siddur*, "The whole concept of constructing a fence around the Torah is rooted in the notion of the vulnerability of spiritual man.... He is easily persuaded, indeed brainwashed, and quickly defeated.... Man sins because he is a weakling, because fate defeats him." The rabbinic control to overcome this human problem did not exist during the days of Adam and Eve.

DID ADAM HAVE AN AFFAIR WITH A DEMON FOR 130 YEARS?

The book of Genesis tells readers that Adam and Eve's first two children were Cain and Abel. Then in Genesis 5:3, it states that when Adam was 130 years old he had his third son Seth. The Bible and Talmud commentator Rashi relied on *Midrash Genesis Rabba* and states that Adam refrained from having sex with Eve for 130 years. The super-commentary on Rashi, *Siftei Chachamim* by the 17th century Polish scholar Shabbetai Bass explains that Rashi said what he said to tell us why the couple had no children for 130 years.

The book *Zohar*, composed by Moses de León around 1280 is filled with supernatural descriptions and events. *Zohar* expands upon the drama. It states that the female demon Lilith who was originally created to be Adam's wife, but whom he rejected and was given Eve in her place, was unable to find another male to help her produce children. She seduced Adam and had a long-standing 130–year relationship with him. Many demons result from the union.[2]

WHAT IS THE MORE REASONABLE EXPLANATION OF THE 130 YEARS?

As I wrote in my book *Mysteries of Judaism I*, it is likely that the early humans did not have exceptionally long lives. The Bible calculates the years differently. The

---

2. See my book *Maimonides: The Exceptional Mind* (Jerusalem: Gefen Publishing House, 2008), for information about Lilith and *Zohar* in the articles, "The Thrice-told Tale of the Likable and Loathsome Lilith" and "Who wrote the *Zohar*?"

average life span before the flood of Noah may not have been hundreds of years, as indicated by a literal reading of the Bible. When the Torah states that Adam lived for 930 years, it may have been referring to years that lasted from one lunar cycle to the next, about 29½ days. If the 930 "years" are divided by twelve (months), the result is 77½ currently-calculated years, which is about the length of lives today. Even if it only took a single day to create the world, Adam would have died when he was 77, and not in his 930th year.

It is also possible that after the flood, the calculation of years changed and people considered the difference from a warm to a cold season as a year, so that two biblical years during this period are equal to one year today. While the Bible states that Abraham lived 175 years, Isaac 180, Joseph 110, and Moses 120, on this basis they would have died at ages 87, 90, 55 and 60, respectively.

This explanation not only explains the seemingly highly unusual lifetime of early biblical figures, but also explains the 130 years before the birth of Seth without the need of the fanciful notions in the Midrashim.

Once this explanation of years is recognized, the lifetime of Adam's years were no longer than months today, so the 130 "years" between the birth of Cain and Able to Seth (130 divided by 12) is a little over ten years, not an unreasonable length of time.

WHAT WAS ADAM'S "SIN"?

In Dr. Cary Schnitzer's book *Understanding Adam's Sin and its Rectification*, Dr. Schnitzer raises interesting questions such as: Why was Adam unable to restrain himself from violating a seemingly trivial commandment? What function did the Tree of Life, which was also in the Garden of Eden with the Tree of Knowledge of Good and Evil, perform?

DR. SCHNITZER FOCUSES ON ADAM'S RELATIONSHIP WITH EVE.

He has fascinating ideas such as Adam fulfilling his life mission when he would feel "such love and concern [for Eve] that, should anything harm her, he would feel as if it harmed him." "Adam's mission was to form a relationship with Eve." "God commanded Adam not to eat from the fruit so that he would cooperate with Eve after she was created." "Only with the presence of another human being could Adam exercise his free will." Adam's terrible error was that he "looked at her as being...his servant." He acted "like a dictator [when he imposed his will] on Eve." When Adam defended himself before God and said, "The woman that you gave to be with me, she gave me the fruit and I ate," he implied that Eve was a being without potential, of little value, and "she deserved death at God's hands." Adam's "sin" was his failure to form a proper relationship with Eve.

Adam, according to Dr. Schnitzer, was not unique in mistakenly mistreating his wife. Abraham also should have consulted with his wife Sarah before taking his son Isaac for sacrification. Had he done so, she would have told him that he misinterpreted God's request. The same for Moses. "Had Moses not separated from [his wife] Zipporah, she almost certainly would have advised him correctly and told him not to send the spies." All too many husbands today are equally foolish, harming themselves, their wives, children, and others.

I agree with Dr. Schnitzer's conclusion. "A person must focus on the good in other people. He must work in partnership with them instead of trying to be an individual superstar or imposing his will on them."

Chapter Four
Cain and Abel

The stories of Cain and Abel are not as simple as people think and the explanations that are given for difficulties are generally mistaken.

WHERE WERE THE WIVES OF CAIN AND ABEL?

In addition to the questions raised in the prior chapters: Why doesn't the Bible mention the birth of the wives of Cain and Abel? What happened to Abel's wife after Cain killed him? What was the mark that God placed on Cain after he killed his brother?[1] We do not know, and despite Midrashim offering clever notions, we will never know. Scripture has many obscurities like these, which we discuss later in this book.

It may satisfy readers to suppose that the story is a myth and myths usually focus only on what is significant. Maimonides states that the story of the eating of the forbidden fruit in Genesis is a myth designed to teach a lesson.[2] So this may also be a myth or a parable.

Alternatively, even if the story is telling actual events of the past, we know that most writers do not reveal every detail that the reader would like to know. To do otherwise would make their tale burdensome, less suspenseful, and possibly boring.

1. Genesis 4:15.
2. Maimonides, *Guide of the Perplexed* 1:2.

MAIMONIDES AND NACHMANIDES

While Maimonides explained many biblical events as visions – meaning human thoughts – he did not belabor the point. Two famed thinkers took extreme positions.

The first well-known Jewish philosopher was Philo of Alexandria, Egypt (c. 20 BCE–50 CE). Philo was the first Jewish philosopher who contributed anything new to Jewish-Greek philosophy. His philosophy incorporated the somewhat mystical views of the ancient Greek philosopher Plato. About forty books that he wrote still exist. They do not offer a systematic philosophy; they are, in essence, a collection of sermons.

Philo was convinced that one should understand the Bible on two levels. The first level contains its literal or plain meaning; words mean what they say. The second, his contribution, is an underlying or allegorical layer, which requires that the alert, more intelligent reader go beyond the obvious and delve deeper into the text. Philo used allegory to interpret virtually everything in Scripture, including names, dates, numbers, and events.

Nachmanides took the opposite approach. He insisted that all events in the Torah and even those in Midrashim were true. They may seem to be impossible to us, such as a talking snake and a talking mule, but God has the power to do what we consider unnatural.[3]

Nachmanides's commentaries to Genesis 11:28 and 32 are excellent examples of his thinking. He retells the imaginative non-biblical legend of Abraham destroying his father's idols (from the Babylonian Talmud, *Bava Batra* 91a), and expands upon the story, giving his original details. He insists that the episode is true and warns us not to be misled by ibn Ezra who argued that the story is a simple legend, a parable invented to teach a moral lesson.

In the 1263 public religious debate with Pablo Christiani before the king in Barcelona, Nachmanides took an opposite approach. Pablo contended that some of the midrashic stories that Nachmanides had insisted were true occurrences

---

3. Moses ben Nachman (Nachmanides), *The Disputation at Barcelona: Ramban,* trans. Rabbi Dr. Charles B. Chavel (BNB Publishing, 2017); Hyam Maccoby, trans. and ed. *Judaism on Trial: Jewish-Christian Disputations in the Middle Ages* (Littman Library of Jewish Civilization in association with Liverpool University Press, 1993).

foreshadowed the birth and mission of Jesus. Nachmanides sidestepped Pablo's trap by disclaiming his belief in the truthfulness and the authority of Midrashim, and said that they are only legends.

Nachmanides's experience shows that the readers may interpret Midrashim in whichever way they want, and one must be careful in explaining them.

Chapter Five
The Patriarchs: Abraham

> Children hear many myths about the patriarchs and as they grow older they continue to believe them even if these myths are untrue.

YOUNG ABRAHAM WAS VERY DIFFERENT THAN WHAT WE THINK

Everything written about Abraham as a young man is midrashic, and everything we learned in elementary school about his early life is wrong. They are imaginative events based on nothing in the Torah. In fact, a close reading of the Torah reveals a totally different young Abraham than the fictional midrashic accounts.

WHAT DOES THE BIBLE SAY ABOUT ABRAHAM'S EARLY LIFE?

The Torah's story of Abraham's early life is brief. It begins in the middle of a chapter, in 11:26, where all that we are told is that Abram, as Abraham was called in his youth, married Sarai, Sarah's early name, and Sarai was barren. Abram's father took his family and left Ur of the Chaldees, without the Bible giving a reason for the trip, came to Haran where the family settled, and then he died. Then, chapter 12 begins to tell events when Abram was seventy-five years old. God spoke to him at that time, with no indication of any prior conversation or relationship. God told him to leave Haran. He obeyed and went to Canaan.

This is all that the Bible tells us about Abraham's early life. Yet there are many imaginative midrashic tales about Abraham's exploits before he is seventy-five years old, which are proven false by other events mentioned in the Bible.

WHERE DOES THE TORAH BEGIN THE ABRAHAM STORY?

Readers may wonder why the Abraham story begins in the middle of a chapter. Christians divided the Bible into chapters, not Jews, although many Jews later accepted many of these chapter divisions. Many of the divisions make no sense, such as this one where Abraham's story begins in the middle of a chapter. Another example is Genesis 1 and 2. Only six of the seven days of creation are in chapter one, with the seventh in chapter two. Chapter 2 should have begun after telling about the creation on the seventh day, with the current verse 2:4, "These are the generations of the heaven and the earth when they were created, in the day that the Lord made earth and heaven."

ABRAHAM DESTROYED HIS FATHER'S IDOLS

Probably the most famous mistaken notion is that the Bible contains the story of Abraham as a youngster convinced that idols are not gods and that the true Deity is unseeable. It is the story of Abraham taking advantage of his father's absence from his store where he sold idols. Abraham, according to the story took a hammer or an ax, and broke all the idols in the store except for one. He placed the hammer or ax in the hand of the remaining whole idol. When his father returned and saw his gods destroyed, Abraham told him that it was clear that the whole idol with the destructing instrument in his hand must have destroyed the other idols because he felt he was the sole god of the world. The midrashic story was invented to belittle idols, to fill in what transpired in Abraham's life during his early years, and to depict Abraham as a devout follower of God. The first mention of Abraham in the Torah is when he is about seventy-five years old. The midrashic story enchants children, most of whom never study the Bible after grade school and think that what they learned as children is a mature vision of Judaism.

Sometime back, I heard a now-retired chief rabbi of Israel say in a sermon that there is a hint of the story in the Torah. Genesis 11:28 and 31 state that Abraham lived in Ur Casdim, translated as "Ur of the Chaldees." The vowel sign indicates that Ur should be sounded as the English word "or," as in black *or* white. It is clear in the context in which the word is mentioned that it is the name of a place.

However, the chief rabbi said that Ur should be pronounced as if the vowel was an *oh*, as in the statement "Oh, my God," which would turn it into the Hebrew word for fire. He argued that the Bible is saying that Abraham left the "fire of the Chaldees," because King Nimrod of the Chaldeans sought to punish Abraham for destroying his father's idols by tossing him into a fiery furnace, but God saved Abraham, and after being saved he left the land of the fire of the Chaldeans.

DID GOD SPEAK TO ABRAHAM AND TELL HIM TO TRAVEL?

In his *Guide of the Perplexed* 2:48, Maimonides states that whenever the Bible or a prophet states that God said something, caused something, or made something,[1] it should be understood that the event occurred by natural means, without the direct involvement of God. Why, then, Maimonides asked, do the Bible and prophets attribute the act to God? He answered, because God made the world and the laws of nature, so, in a sense, God is the ultimate cause of the event. Thus, the biblical statement that God told Abraham to leave his home and go elsewhere means that after some reflection and, perhaps, after some now unknown occurrence or goal, Abraham decided that he and his family needed a change of residence.

SOME OTHER RABBINICAL IMAGINATIVE NOTIONS ABOUT ABRAHAM

Numerous claims made about Abraham are most likely to enhance his stature, reputation, distinction, and prestige. Perhaps also because it was felt that Abraham must have had some kind of relationship with God before he was seventy-five years old.[2] These views are not even hinted at in the Torah.

Many people think that Abraham was the first Jew and was the first to recognize the existence of God. He was the first to convert people to have a relationship with God and even watched for passing wayfarers whom he could welcome, feed, and then speak with them about God.

His father sold idols and Abraham as a child destroyed them, got into trou-

---

1. As when Joseph told his brothers in Genesis 45:7, "God sent me before you." Or in Genesis 24:51 when Laban told Abraham's servant regarding Rebekah, "Let her be a wife to the son of your master, as the Lord spoke." Or in Jonah 2:11, "The Lord spoke to the fish and it vomited out Jonah."

2. My father Rabbi Dr. Nathan Drazin wrote a book for children based on the Midrash called *Midrash Rabbah and Other Midrashim*, which has these imaginative allegations. This is a fit book for children as Dad intended, on the same level as Alibaba and the Forty Thieves. I just edited and published this book with a foreword about my parents.

ble with King Nimrod who had him tossed into a fiery furnace from which God miraculously saved him.

When Abraham went to war against four kings who kidnapped his nephew Lot, he tossed sticks and sand, which turned into swords and arrows, and killed them.

He and his servant Eliezer were so physically strong that when the Torah states that Abraham went to war against the four kings with 318, it means that just Abraham and Eliezer fought the four kings. The numerical value of the Hebrew letters spelling Eliezer's name total 318.

Abraham brought back men and women from the war, but not children, because the children freed themselves when they saw Abraham and became proselytes.

MELCHIZEDEK WAS SUPERIOR TO ABRAHAM

While there were rabbis who extolled Abraham as indicated above, other rabbis gave a contrary interpretation, also not mentioned in the Bible, showing that the king and priest Melchizedek who came to Abraham in Genesis 14 was superior to the patriarch.

For example, these rabbis wrote in Midrashim that Melchizedek was called King of Shalem, Shalem means whole, and the title King of Shalem is suggesting that Melchizedek was such a holy man that he was born circumcised.[3]

They say that the reference to Melchizedek bringing bread and wine to Abraham when he returned after fighting and beating four kings means Melchizedek revealed Torah to Abraham.

One rabbi even added that Melchizedek was responsible for the wealth that the patriarchs enjoyed. When the Bible states that Melchizedek gave the other, "a tenth of all" the rabbi explained that he blessed Abraham with riches, so much so that even his son Isaac and grandson Jacob enjoyed prosperity.

THE BIBLE ITSELF NEGATES THESE CLAIMS

Besides the fact that none of these fascinating fables are even hinted at in the Bible, a close reading of the Torah text shows that they are untrue. One example is the well-known tale that Abraham's father made and sold idols, Abraham destroyed

3. The same claim is made about Moses and some other famous people.

them, his father complained to King Nimrod, and the king tossed Abraham into a fiery furnace. There is no indication that Abraham had any conflict with his father Terah. The opposite is true.

As stated earlier, the only information about Abraham's life before age seventy-five is in Genesis 11. That chapter states that Abraham's father took his family and left Ur of the Chaldees, came to Haran where the family settled, and Abraham's father died there. What we see is a dutiful son who had an apparently good relationship with his dad. He then took his wife and went with his father when he decided to resettle in a different country and into a different culture. Abraham was only seventy-five when he left his father.

The rabbis noted that Genesis 11 states that Terah died and Genesis 12 tells about Abraham leaving Haran for Canaan. The order of these verses seems to indicate that Abraham did not leave his father until he died. However, the rabbis point out that Terah was still alive when Abraham at age seventy-five finally decided to leave home. The Bible states that Terah was seventy years old when he begot Abram and he lived until age 205. Simple math reveals that Terah was 145 years old (70 when Abraham was born plus 75 when Abraham left home) and lived another sixty years after Abraham left (205 minus 145). Why, ask the rabbis, does the Bible report that Terah died before Abraham left? They reply, so as not to disparage Abraham by depicting him abandoning his aged father. This is another indication that the Torah was depicting a good relationship between Abraham and his dad.

WAS ABRAHAM THE FIRST JEW?

There are three conflicting ways that many Jews view Abraham. Some say that he was the first Jew. They feel that Abraham introduced the concept of God to humanity. They forget that Adam and Noah also had dealings with God. They do not know that the noun, "Jew" is not in the Bible. It is a term used to describe the people after the northern country was conquered. The ten tribes who inhabited the northern country disappeared, and the remaining people in the south of the land were primarily from the tribe of Judah. The land was called Judea, and the people Judeans, Jews for short.[4]

---

4. The Israelites were united under kings Saul, David, and Solomon, but split around 920 BCE

Abraham was not the first Jew. Judaism did not exist during the days of the patriarchs. The Torah does not say this. What it says is that Abraham will be the ancestor of many nations and the forerunner of a great people.

Also, by paying attention to what the Bible writes, we see that many people knew about the existence of God long before Abraham.

Adam, Eve, and Cain spoke with God. Noah the ancestor of all humanity spoke with God and he and his son Shem were still alive during a large part of Abraham's lifetime.

If Abraham accepted Melchizedek as Noah's son Shem who was a king as well as a priest, as many rabbis claim, then Abraham was not the first to recognize God. He was quite possibly subservient to Shem/Melchizedek who had a ceremonial and sacramental connection to God.

AN ALTERNATIVE INTERPRETATION

As previously stated, it is possible that many of the legends about Abraham were to explain what he did during the first seventy-five years of his life. This is a long time, and a man like Abraham must have done many great things before he reached age seventy-five.

However, using the calculations shown previously in chapter 3 (What Is the More Reasonable Explanation of the 130 Years?) we recognize that Abraham was thirty-seven years old when he left Haran with his wife and nephew and moved to Canaan. This is a typical age when men seek a new path of life, restarting his and his family's life in a new land. It is therefore possible that for the thirty-seven years until he sought this change, Abraham did not do anything extraordinary.

Reading the Bible in this fashion, we see that Noah and Shem were alive during the early lifetime of Abraham and they knew about God before him. Genesis 9:28 states that Noah lived 350 years after the flood. Using the biblical calendar called anno mundi, the years of the world, the calendar based on biblical accounts, the Flood occurred in 1656 anno mundi. Noah therefore died in 2006. Abraham was born in 1948 anno mundi and was fifty-eight years old when Noah died.

---

into two kingdoms, Israel in the north and Judea in the south. Israel was conquered in 720 BCE and Judea in 586 BCE. Israel never revived, but Judea did around 536 BCE and was defeated by the Romans in 70 CE.

Genesis 11:10–11 states that Shem was one hundred years old when he bore his first son, and this occurred two years after the Flood, and Shem lived another five hundred years after he bore his son. Shem died in 2258 anno mundi. So, Shem was alive for 310 years after Abraham's birth.

Looking at Abraham's life in this way in that he was not unusually old, he serves as a model for all of us today, men and women. As we mature and begin to understand better the world and our responsibilities, we, like Abraham can change.

When Abraham came to the new land, to Canaan, later called Israel, he had a vision of future success. Genesis 12:7 tells us his first reaction. "The Lord appeared to Abram and said: 'I will give this land to your descendants.' And he built there an altar for the Lord who appeared to him." At age thirty-seven, he created a new life.

Chapter Six
The Patriarchs: Isaac

We know very little about Abraham's son Isaac. He is almost a nonentity. In a Hebrew school, the children were told to paint pictures of the patriarchs. One child used colors for all of them except for Isaac, who he painted white.

DID THE STORY OF THE NEAR SACRIFICE OF ISAAC ACTUALLY HAPPEN?

I find it hard to accept that God, who is all-knowing, needed to test Abraham to discover if he would do all that God required of him. I also find it difficult to accept the midrashic idea that God wanted Abraham to act as he did as a lesson for Abraham's descendants on how to behave. One of the reasons for my view is that it does not seem reasonable that a loving God would place the family in such a situation, with all the pain and anguish that Abraham, Isaac, and Sarah must have suffered. Also, why didn't Abraham object to the murder of his son as he did to the murder of the citizens of Sodom and Gomorrah?

In his *Guide of the Perplexed* 2:48 and 3:24, Maimonides explains what the Torah means when it states that God did or said something (2:48), and the six instances where the Torah tells us that God placed people in a trial (3:24). He writes that God has no need or desire to hurt people with trials. This is a natural phenomenon; it is normal for people to go through difficult times. The individuals should learn from their experience to improve and live a satisfactory life.

MY UNDERSTANDING

I understand that Abraham lived when people had unusual behaviors that they felt they needed to do to satisfy their god or gods. One way, of course, was the idea that the gods wanted people to kill the animals whom they had created and burn the carcasses on altars with the idea that despite the animal being turned into smoke the god would enjoy eating it. Another idea was to give the gods what they loved most – their child.

Abraham loved God and wondered if the general population was correct and he should show his love by sacrificing Isaac. He never put his idea into practice. What we read is either his nighttime dream concerning his dilemma, or a daytime reflection. He thinks of sacrificing his son, even needing to tie him up to get it done. Then, an angel comes and tells him God does not want the sacrifice, that as he is about to copy the mass behavior, his intelligence (angel) told him that this was wrong.

HOW OLD WAS ISAAC WHEN HIS FATHER TOOK HIM TO BE SACRIFICED?

If we take the story as factual, some questions arise such as how old Isaac was at that time?

Some rabbis who calculated the years according to the literal reading of the Bible text, concluded that Isaac was thirty-seven years old when Abraham took him to be sacrificed because of what he understood as God's decree. The question raised is why a thirty-seven-year-old Isaac would allow his 137-year-old father to kill him.

If we use the calculations above, and divide these numbers by two, then it becomes clear that Isaac at that time was only about eighteen years old and his father about sixty-eight. There are, as previously noted, some rabbis who say that Isaac was thirty-seven and others who say he was much younger.

WAS ISAAC EXTREMELY ANGRY THAT ABRAHAM TRIED TO KILL HIM?

Some people think that Isaac was angry with his father because he lied to him about the two going on a trip to offer a sacrifice to God. He understood his father saying the sacrifice would be an animal, but then his father tied him up on top of a stone altar where he planned to kill him, and only stopped when he heard a voice from heaven telling him to desist.

They assume that Isaac ran off from his father and did not return home with him. They base their view on the wording of Genesis 22:19, "Abraham returned to his young men, and they rose up and went together to Beersheba, and Abraham dwelt in Beersheba." Isaac is not mentioned with Abraham when he "returned to his young men." Nor is he mentioned dwelling with his father in Beersheba.

This negative reading of 22:19 that Isaac left his father very angry is at odds with later events in Genesis, which show that Abraham and Isaac had a good relationship.

Genesis 24, which describes an event after the Akedah (the name given to the near sacrifice of Isaac, meaning "binding [of Isaac]") tells that Abraham sent his most loyal servant to his relatives in his former homeland to bring back a wife for Isaac. This chapter suggests that father and son were friendly and that Abraham was trying to help Isaac.

The last sentence of chapter 24 reinforces this conclusion. It states that Isaac lived with his new wife in his now-deceased mother Sara's tent, which we can safely assume was near Abraham's tent. So, we see father and son living together.

Following Genesis 24, chapter 25 tells about Abraham's death and in verse 9, it states that Isaac and his half-brother Ishmael buried Abraham in the Cave of Machpelah, which, again, seems to indicate that Isaac had no conflict with his father.

We have no way of knowing about Isaac's emotional reactions to his father obeying what he understood as a divine command in the Torah verses. But we are able to see that there are no indications in any verse other than what is read into 22:19 that Isaac harbored ill will against his father, and when Isaac is mentioned after the Akedah, we see him interacting with Abraham in a positive manner.

HOW DOES THE MIDRASHIC LITERATURE TREAT ISAAC'S BEHAVIOR AFTER THE AKEDAH?

The Babylonian Talmud, *Sotah* 14a states, "the Holy One, blessed be he, comforted mourners, for it is written, 'And it came to pass after the death of Abraham, that God blessed Isaac his son,' so do thou also comfort mourners."[1] It is clear that the Talmudic rabbis felt that Isaac loved his father and needed comfort.

Rabbi Isaac states in *Midrash Rabba Genesis*[2] that when Isaac saw his father about to sacrifice him, he said that since he was young, he feared he might tremble when he saw the knife "and I will grieve thee, whereby the slaughter may be

1. Isidore Epstein, *The Babylonian Talmud, Seder Nashim* in four volumes, volume III (London: Soncino Press, 1938), commenting on Genesis 25:11.
2. Harry Freedman, trans. *Midrash Rabbah: Genesis II* (London: The Soncino Press, 1983).

rendered unfit and this will not count as a real sacrifice; therefore bind me very firmly." This Midrash states that Isaac agreed to be sacrificed and even to be bound, and was not angry that his father wanted to kill him.

It asks our question, "Where was Isaac?" It answers, "Rabbi Berekiah said in the name of the rabbis of the other place:[3] He [Abraham] sent him to Shem [Noah's son] to study Torah... Rabbi Jose ben Rabbi Hanina said: He sent him [home] at night, for fear of the [evil] eye." These rabbis agree that Isaac did not go home with his father, but it was not because he hated him.

Thus, the interpretation that Isaac hated his father is incorrect.

3. A note in the translation explains that the reference is to Babylon.

Chapter Seven
The Patriarchs: Jacob

Jacob's life was full of fascinating events. In his younger years, he was involved in several deceptions. One of his adventures concerns a wrestling contest that Scripture describes hyperbolically as continuing for an entire night. Did it really occur at all? Who was the person with whom Jacob wrestled?

DID JACOB WRESTLE WITH AN ANGEL?

My father Rabbi Dr. Nathan Drazin was a very wise man. He was a rabbi in Shaarei Tfiloh Congregation in Baltimore, Maryland for 31 years, and I enjoyed listening to his sermons. The one I liked the best concerned his true interpretation of the incident where many mistakenly understand that Jacob wrestled with an angel. What really happened that night?

The story is in Genesis 32:23–33. Previously, Jacob's mother Rebekah heard that her husband Isaac intended to give their son Esau a very favorable blessing after Esau would hunt an animal and prepare it as a meal for his father. Rebekah preferred that her husband's blessing be given to Jacob and persuaded Jacob to deceive his father Isaac who was virtually blind, say he was Esau, and take the blessing.

(To understand the story, and some other similar stories about oaths, curses, and blessings, one needs to understand that in ancient times, people believed that once a person uttered an oath, curse, or blessing, it was impossible to annul it. Thus, once Isaac gave Jacob the blessing in Genesis 27, even though done fraudulently, it was effective, and Esau could not get it. Another example is the case of Jephthah in Judges 11:30–31 when he vowed that if victorious in his upcoming battle, "that whatsoever comes out of the doors of my house to meet me when I return in peace... I will offer up for a burnt offering." Although he never expected that it would be his only child, his daughter, who greeted him, and this was clearly a mistaken vow, he was stuck, and had to offer his daughter as a sacrifice. Later, in post-biblical times, the rabbis changed the rule, and set up ways to annul vows, blessings, and curses.)

Jacob accepted his mother's advice, deceived his father, and secured the blessing. When Esau returned with the food his father requested, he heard what Jacob did, cried, begged his father for a blessing, and was told that his father could not annul what he had done. In Genesis 27:41, Esau "said in his heart, when the days of mourning for my father arise, I will kill my brother Jacob." Rebekah could not hear what Esau was thinking, but she saw his hatred. She advised Jacob to leave the country, go to the home of her brother Laban, and stay there until Esau's anger cooled. Jacob did so. He stayed with Laban for about twenty years. Genesis 32:23–33 tells about an incident during his return after the twenty-year absence. Expecting an encounter with Esau the next day or very soon, he organized his family and wealth to appease his brother or face his attack. Then he placed his family on one side of the Wadi Jabbok and remained alone on the other side.

The Bible tells us that he wrestled that night with a man until daybreak. The Bible does not identify the man. During the battle, the man strained Jacob's thigh. He asked Jacob to release him. Jacob said he would do so if the man blessed him. The man said, "What is your name?" Jacob replied, "Jacob." The man said, "You will no longer be called Jacob, but Israel, because you strove with God and men and prevailed." The Bible continues: "And he blessed him there," without clarifying if the discussion about his name was the blessing, or if the man added a blessing. Then Jacob calls the name of the place Peniel, a word meaning, "face of God," and remarks "I have seen God face-to-face, and my life is preserved." Thereafter, Jacob limped.

While the end text speaks about Jacob striving with God, there is no mention of it in the chapter. Nor is there mention of Jacob striving with men, only one man. Nor is there indication other than Jacob's statement that he saw God face-to-face. How should we understand these statements? Even more significantly, how should we understand the entire incident? Why did the fight occur? Who was the man? What connection does this battle have to do with Esau wanting to kill Jacob? What is the significance of Jacob limping after the battle? Do all Bible commentators agree what occurred?

THERE ARE DIFFERENT VIEWS ON THE SUBJECT.

The prophet Hosea, in 12:4–5, stated that "by his strength, he [Jacob] strove with a godlike being; he strove with an angel and prevailed. He wept and made a supplication to him." Hosea also states that Jacob had previously held onto Esau's foot in the womb.

Obviously, no one could know what transpired in a woman's womb, and holding his brother's foot, like the rest of what Hosea says, is pure poetry, Midrash, and hyperbole, and is not meant to be taken literally.

Rashi was convinced that both angels and demons exist. For example: Relying on the Babylonian Talmud, *Chagigah* 16a, Rashi writes in his commentary to Genesis 6:19 that Noah saved the demons in his ark along with his family and animals. In Genesis 32:4, Rashi writes that Jacob used heavenly angels as messengers to his brother Esau carrying gifts to him. Relying on *Midrash Genesis Rabba,* Rashi states in 32:25 that the "man" with whom Jacob wrestled was the angel who protected his brother Esau.

Maimonides, who did not believe that God needed an army of superhuman beings to accomplish the divine purposes, wrote that beings called angels do not exist; an angel is anything that accomplishes the divine purpose, such as the wind, snow, rain, and even humans that act as God wants. In his *Guide of the Perplexed* 3:42, he writes that the events of Genesis 32:23–33 did not really happen; "it was entirely a prophetic vision." He also writes that the biblical story of Balaam and the speaking ass where an angel speaks to Balaam was "a prophetic vision," and he gives other examples.

My father explained that Jacob returned home after an absence of some twenty years and was very frightened that his brother Esau would seize the opportunity to kill him. His fear affected his sleep. He dreamed that he was wrestling with a man. Would he be victorious and stay alive as he hoped in his encounter with Esau? In the dream, the man gives him confidence, and reminds Jacob that he had been successful in the past; "you strove with God and men and prevailed." He is not referring to the wrestling that night.

When did Jacob strive with God? It was in Genesis 28 during his flight from his home toward the home of Laban, his mother's brother. He was also frightened that night and had a dream. In the dream he strove/negotiated with God. He laid out five conditions and said, if these conditions are fulfilled, "then shall the Lord be my God." The conditions were successful, so he would also be successful.

When did Jacob strive with men? Many times. He did so twice with Esau. First when Esau came to him hungry and gave up his birthright in order to have some food, and later when Isaac wanted to bless Esau and Jacob stole the blessing. Then, repeatedly he strove with his father-in-law Laban. He was successful in each instance. So, he received assurances in his dream.

My father pointed out that Don Isaac Abarbanel (also spelled Abravenel) strongly disagreed.[1] He argued that since the Bible does not say Jacob had a dream, the wrestling with the angel was an actual event. Besides, he insisted, the Bible states that Jacob limped after the encounter; why would a person limp after a dream? My father, who had an MA in psychology in addition to his PhD, explained that despite his wide reading, Abarbanel ignored the fact that some vivid traumatic dreams are so impactful that people feel the hurt experienced in the dream, at least for a little while, upon awaking.

In short, Maimonides tells us that Jacob did not fight with an angel. They do not exist. And if they did, it would have been impossible to fight one of them during an entire night and beat it.

In essence, the story of Jacob wrestling during the night was an internal struggle just as Abraham had at the Akedah.

DID JACOB GIVE HIS SON "A COAT OF MANY COLORS"?

It is likely that this is a mistranslation of Genesis 37:3 which states in Hebrew that Jacob gave his son Joseph a *ketonet passim*. The noun *ketonet* does mean a coat or shirt, but *passim* usually means striped. Thus, "a coat of many colors" is a conjecture.

---

1. Zev Bar Eitan, *Abravanel's World of Torah: A Structured Interpretation* (Renaissance Torah Press, 2012).

Chapter Eight
The Patriarch's Children

There are not only misconceptions about the creation of the world, the early humans, and the patriarchs, but many people also have wrong ideas about the descendants of the patriarchs.

THE TORAH DOES NOT PORTRAY ISHMAEL AND ESAU AS BAD MEN

There is no evidence anywhere in the Bible suggesting that Abraham's son Ishmael and Isaac's son Esau were bad people. It was only in post-biblical times that Jews made the erroneous claim about them. While the rabbis probably did not initiate this false notion, they accepted it, as they accepted many practices begun by average Jews, such as the Tashlich ceremony.[1] This is unfortunate both because it is slanderous and violates the Torah's teaching to tell the truth and not disparage people, but it also exasperated relationships between Jews, Moslems, and Christians since tradition arose among the people that Moslems were descendant from Ishmael and Christians from Esau.

ISHMAEL

Genesis 16:10–16 has a tale that an angel appeared to Hagar, foretelling that she would have a son, a prediction that paralleled the prophecy of the birth of Isaac.

1. Drazin, *Maimonides: The Exceptional Mind*. This book discusses the origin of Tashlich and other superstitious practices started by the average public, not the rabbis who opposed the practice at first, until they changed it. The chapter is entitled: "The Tashlich Ceremony: Another Bribe to Silence Satan."

The Bible tells us that Abraham loved Ishmael. In Genesis 17:18, he begged God to consider Ishmael worthy to succeed him, for he did not need another son. Soon, Isaac was born, and Sarah became very protective of him. She saw Ishmael playing with Isaac, and while the text states that Ishmael and Isaac *metzacheik*, meaning "having fun together," Rashi to 21:9 interprets the Hebrew word *metzacheik* differently. While the root is the same as the root in Isaac's name *tz-ch-k*, and means "laughter," "joy," with the post-biblical view of Ishmael in his commentary, Rashi argues that it implies "incest," "murder," "quarrel," and imagines that Ishmael shot arrows at Isaac to kill him. Sarah anxiously, repeating words twice, tells her husband, "Cast out the bondwoman [Hagar] and her son; so that he not be an heir, the son of this bondwoman, with my son, with Isaac."

What Abraham heard "concerning his son" deeply saddened him. He agreed to accept Sarah's demand only when God told him to do so and assured him that he would take care of Ishmael by making him into a nation. Still upset, *Midrash Genesis Rabba* 53:17 imagines that Sarah cast an evil eye on Ishmael while he was leaving, and his mother Hagar had to carry him. Abraham was grieved that he had to leave.

After Hagar and Ishmael left, an angel appeared to Hagar a second time and assured her that God said, "I will make him a great nation." And the Torah states, "God was with the lad." Later, when Abraham died, Ishmael joined his brother Isaac and the two buried their father in the cave of Machpelah (25:9). The second-century book Jubilees 22 states that Isaac and Ishmael got on well together; they celebrated the holiday of Shavuot together. There is nothing in this tale that disparages Ishmael.

Jews even called their sons Ishmael among other names in the early years of the first millennium. The famed colleague of Rabbi Akiva around 135 CE was Rabbi Ishmael.[2]

ESAU

Esau's story is similar to Ishmael's. His mother received a prophecy before his birth that she would bear twins. They will be two people and the elder will serve

2. In contrast, Jews did not call their sons Esau during this period. As we will see, the disparagement of Esau began early, and that of Ishmael, many centuries later.

the younger (25:23). Esau exited his mother first, and it was Jacob right from the womb who began the strife with Esau; he held Esau's heel presumably, according to Midrashim, to stop him from being the first-born (25:26). Isaac saw no fault in Esau and loved him better than Jacob, but Rebekah loved Jacob more (25:28). When Esau returned from the field one day very hungry while Jacob was making pottage, he requested some, but Jacob refused to give him any unless Esau sell him his birthright. Esau did so without any complaints (25:29–34). Later, when Isaac wanted to bless Esau and Jacob stole the blessing (27:1–41), Esau was very hurt, angry, cried, and even thought to kill Jacob, but only after his father's death so that he would not grieve him. However, Jacob fled in fear. Esau, perhaps forgetting his anger, did not pursue Jacob. Some twenty years later when Jacob returned, Esau greeted him. He ran to him, embraced him, fell on his neck, kissed him, and they wept together (33:4). There is nothing in this tale that indicates Esau did wrong.

WHEN DID JEWISH ANCESTORS BEGIN TO VIEW ISHMAEL AND ESAU UNFAVORABLY?

While the historical origins of this thought are unknown, the consensus is that the disparagement of biblical Ishmael began when Moslem hoards invaded and conquered Israel in the seventh century. Jews identified the Moslems as descendants of Ishmael. The Jewish masses displaced their hatred of the invaders upon Abraham's son. The rabbis accepted the identification and continued it in many of their writings.[3]

The false testimony about Esau may have begun either because of the mistreatment of Jews by Romans or by the early Christians. The Roman general Pompey entered Israel in 63 BCE and soon thereafter, the Romans incorporated Israel into the Roman Empire and mistreated the Jews. The first Christians were Jewish and differed with their coreligionists only in giving Jesus some special powers or authority – what this was in the early days, differed among the Christians. Later, especially by the time that the Romans destroyed the temple, the Jews and Chris-

3. *Jewish Bible Quarterly* 28:1 (2000).

tians became unfriendly to each other, many Christians sided with the Romans and did not help fellow Jews. Soon Jews began to use the name Esau to identify both Rome and Christians.[4]

4. Paul, in his book Romans, quoted an unnamed source with God saying, "Jacob I loved but Esau I hated." This should not be taken as an early belittling, mocking, or even criticism of the biblical Esau. Paul at that time was attempting to convert non-Jews to Judaism. He was saying in a hyperbolic manner that when God promised great glory to Abraham's and Isaac's descendants, God was not promising to give it to all of their descendants, but only to the offspring of Jacob, not Esau.

Chapter Nine
Similar Stories to Those Told About the Patriarchs

Comparing stories told in Genesis about the patriarchs with other biblical stories about other men and women will enhance and deepen our understanding of both stories.

RELATED TALES

Many tales about Abraham have parallels with other biblical figures and their stories in other biblical books. For example, Genesis 18 begins with a story about three men/angels that inform Abraham that he will have a son. One angel also tells Samson's parents, in Judges 13, that he would be born, and the New Testament (Luke 1:30–31) has one angel foretell the birth of Jesus. Abraham received the message because he was an old man and the birth was unusual. Why foretell the other births? In the Abraham story, is the visit of three angels significant? Why three?

In chapter 18 Abraham pleads with God to save the cities of Sodom and Gomorrah if ten righteous people are found in them. Why ten? In chapter 14, Abraham saves the two cities when they have only one family, that of his nephew Lot, less than ten people. Is there a difference?

In Jeremiah 5:1, the prophet predicts that the destruction of Jerusalem would happen "if you can find a man, if there is one who does justice and seeks truth." Why does Jeremiah focus on truth rather than righteousness? Why is one man sufficient to save Jerusalem? Why is Jonah upset when he finds an entire city of Nineveh having righteous people.

In chapter 22, Abraham refrains from sacrificing his son Isaac. He didn't follow the religious practice of his age where such sacrifices were de rigueur. Yet, his descendants continued to sacrifice their children. Judges 11 tells how the judge Jephthah sacrificed his daughter by burning her, or confining her for life in a type of monastery, but the text is obscure. Jeremiah 7:31 testifies to the Israelites burning their sons and daughters. The New Testament states that God sacrificed his son. Some scholars argue that the Jewish practice of pidyon haben, where parents pay a kohen, a descendant of the ancient priestly caste, to redeem a firstborn son, shows the discomfort Jews must have felt at one time about discontinuing the sacrifice to God. Why did human sacrifices continue after Abraham showed it was wrong?

God "tests" both Abraham and Job, but Abraham's test involved human sacrifices and Job's involved the challenge of why good people suffer. Is there a connection?

The Bible doesn't show God and Isaac speaking ever again to Abraham after the event of the near sacrifice of Isaac. Why were both silent? Is there a connection between God and Isaac?

A FEW OTHER POINTS ABOUT ABRAHAM IN THESE CHAPTERS

Chapter 18 relates that God visited Abraham, and then states that three men arrived. Verse 22 states that the three visitors "turned from there, and went toward Sodom; but Abraham remained before the Lord." The sages in *Midrash Sifrei* 4 note that obviously the verse is saying that God remained with Abraham for Abraham left to greet the three strangers. The Midrash interprets this as one of eighteen verses that the ancients rewrote to protect God's honor; God is not like a servant who waits on a master. They called the eighteen *tikkun soferim,* scribal changes. The rabbis are saying that our Torah is not like the original Torah.

In 22:7, Abraham is called a *navi* (prophet). Yet 1 Samuel 9:9 states that the term *navi* was not in use before the days of the judge Samuel; such people were called *ro'im* (seers), during the earlier period. Arnold Ehrlich argues that the usage of *navi* proves that the composition of this part of Genesis occurred during, or after the time of Samuel, centuries after Moses. Is he right?

Chapter Ten
Moses

> While the Torah explains why Moses was given this name, it is possible, even likely, that this explanation was stated to enhance the near miraculous nature of the story and God's involvement in saving Moses. Additionally, a famous misunderstanding of an episode involving Moses led many Jews to think that Moses disobeyed God's command.

MOSES'S NAME

It is unlikely that Pharaoh's daughter gave Moses a Hebrew name in Exodus 2:10 meaning "draw out" because she rescued a Hebrew child from drawing in water. She most likely did not know Hebrew and would not want to emphasize that she was disobeying her father who wanted all male Israelites killed.

The Egyptian word *msy* means "born" and was used by many Egyptians such as Thutmose and Ramose. Therefore, in all likelihood, the name is Egyptian.

MOSES HITTING THE ROCK TO PRODUCE WATER FOR THE ISRAELITES

Another misunderstanding most likely exists in the story in Exodus 17 and Numbers 20. It is about an event happening in a place later called Meribah, meaning "strife," because the Israelites complained to Moses that they needed water and Moses enquired of God what to do. In both tellings of the tale, God instructs Moses to take his staff with him and go to a rock. In Exodus, God instructs Moses to hit the rock. In Numbers, God told him to speak to the rock. After Moses hit the rock twice in Numbers, God says to Moses, "Because you did not act properly to sanctify me before the Israelites, you will not bring them into the land that I gave them."

Many understand that the Bible is relating two separate events, not a retelling of a single event. They interpret the Numbers version as stating that God punished Moses because he struck the rock rather than speaking to it as God instructed. They ignore that God told Moses to take his staff with him and believe that speaking to the rock would have produced a more startling miracle than hitting the rock.

This is an error. There are not two stories but one. In both tellings, God told Moses to take his staff with him, obviously to use it to hit the rock. In the first Exodus telling Moses hit the rock and God does not berate Moses because he did what God wanted. It is baseless to presume that God was satisfied once when Moses hit the rock but not the second time in Numbers when God told Moses to speak to the rock. This is one event. In both versions, God told Moses to take his staff with him. The additional instruction placed in the second version is the common biblical narrative technique to add information when a story repeats. We do not know what "speak to the rock" implies. It may simply be, tell the Israelites what you are about to do. We also do not know what Moses did wrong. It was most likely his calling the people "rebels" in Numbers 20:11, this lack of control, this outburst, showed that Moses in his old age was no longer fit to lead the people

RELYING ON DIVINE HELP

Chapter Eleven
Jerusalem, the Place Chosen by God

Most people are convinced that God chose Jerusalem as the holy city and place to offer sacrifices. Actually, the Pentateuch, the Five Books of Moses, does not explicitly identify Jerusalem as a holy city, or the place for the temple. As indicated in II Samuel 5:6–9, David conquered Jerusalem and made it his capital for apparently strategic reasons: It was located at the midpoint between the southern and northern tribes. David had ruled as king over the southern tribes and now wanted to unite the tribes. Deep valleys surrounded the city, and it had plenty of water that made it a natural fortress.

THE BIBLICAL LAW ABOUT THE PLACE FOR SACRIFICES

Deuteronomy 12:11 establishes worship places "at the site that *Y-H-V-H*, your God, will choose." The location is unknown here or elsewhere in the Torah.[1]

Significantly, the altar was located in several different places before Jerusalem without any prophet or even the Bible itself stating that the placement was a violation of the biblical mandate.

1. Deuteronomy 27:5–7 requires building an altar and offering sacrifices to God on Mount Ebal after the Israelites first entered Canaan, which Joshua did in Joshua 8:30–32.

1. There are close to two dozen similar commands with just small changes in the language, such as Deuteronomy 12:14, 21; 14:23, 24; and 16:16.

2. Later, Shiloh was the place to bring sacrifices[2] until its destruction by the Philistines after serving as the place for sacrifices for 369 years. The High Priest Eli officiated there until he died during the Philistine attack. The prophet Samuel also officiated there.[3]
3. Sacrifices took place in Kiryat-yearim for twenty years after Shiloh until the ark came to Jerusalem.[4]

RABBINICAL UNDERSTANDING

The rabbis justified the actions. *Midrash Mekhilta de R. Ishmael* states in Pasch 1 that the Israelites could establish altars anywhere until Jerusalem became the only site for sacrifices. Afterwards, according to the rabbis, Jerusalem was the only place to make sacrifices. Similarly, the Mishnah *Zevachim* 14:4–8 has the rabbinical view of building altars at local "high places," but only when there was no tabernacle, and no altar at Shiloh and Jerusalem.

REASON FOR THE MANDATE

Although, as Maimonides teaches, God neither needs, nor desires sacrifices and only "allowed" them because the Israelites at the time felt this was the way of showing love and respect to God, the Bible gave much space to many laws regulating the sacrifices. This was to control the frequent overzealous nature of many people with regard to religion and the natural inclination of people to copy the behavior of others, especially people such as religious leaders of other religions. Thus, there are biblical rules restricting the offering of certain animals, such as lions, and there were controlled times that sacrifices could be brought, and even limited when the Israelites could enter the temple by means of impurity laws.[5]

IN SUMMARY

Since sacrifices took place in various locations for about four centuries, it is reasonable to understand that the repeated mandate to offer sacrifices only at places

---

2. As indicated in Joshua 18:1, Judges 21:19, and Samuel 1:30.
3. The number of years is the opinion in the Babylonian Talmud, *Zevachim* 118b.
4. Samuel 7:2.
5. In *Guide of the Perplexed* 3:32, Maimonides explains that certainly objects that are otherwise clean and dead bodies do not make a person impure; the laws were developed simply to limit the times that the Israelites could visit the tabernacle and temple.

of God's choosing, and without designating a specific place of choice, allowed the Israelites the option of which place to select for the offerings. The statement "that God will choose" should most likely be understood that God will let it be known after humans make the selection if God is satisfied with the choice.

Chapter Twelve
The Meaning and Purpose of Prayers

Most people do not know how to daven, or how to read the prayers. They speed through them as if they are in a speed-reading course. They have no, or very little understanding of what they are reading and do not attempt to understand the prayers, their history, theology, philosophy, why they need to say them, and what impact the prayers should have on their lives. Whether or not God listens to prayers and whether or not God responds to them, the purpose of prayers is human- not God-oriented.

PRAYERS ARE MEANT TO ENCOURAGE JEWS TO JUDGE THEMSELVES

The Hebrew word for the verb "to pray," *l'hitpaleil,* means literally "to judge oneself." The three-letter root of the word is *p-l-l,* which means "judge." The Hebrew term is reflexive, called the *hitpa'el* form, it refers back to the person, meaning that verb is not directed to the outside. The purpose of prayer, even when the wording may seem addressed to God, is to improve the person praying by prompting him to think about what he is reading, to judge himself based on what is being read, to understand the general teachings of Judaism, the decision to improve, and how to do it, then to do it. It is not a pseudo-speed-reading course. Its goal is not to finish a specific reading in the synagogue or at home. The goal is to stimulate actions.

ORIGIN OF PRAYERS

The weekday and Shabbat siddur (prayer book), and the festival machzors, which are also prayer books,[1] are not what people think. They are not a collection of

1. Originally all the prayers were placed in a single book. But after more and more prayers

material that teaches Jewish ideas and values. They are a compendium of materials from various sources added by various groups during different periods, often containing conflicting views.

There is both rational and mystical material in these books, such as a rather long quote from the mystical book *Zohar*, recited when one removes the Torah from the ark and another prayer mystically describing God wearing tefillin. There are also historical statements that are no longer applicable today and which many Jews reject such as the prayer for the restoration of sacrifices and thanking God for not making the reciter a woman. Pious and respected mystics instituted many prayers and practices. Non-mystics saw these pious people saying the prayers and doing the acts and thought that what they heard and saw was a good religious idea, so without knowing why the mystics initiated what they did, they followed the action of the mystics.

Although a rational person would reject the ideas in the cited examples, they should make readers think about their concept of God, history, how history changes, why it changes, their concept of equality, and more.

FRIDAY NIGHT'S KABBALAT SHABBAT CEREMONY AND LECHA DODI

A good example of the above is the Friday night service just before the traditional Maariv prayers when one recites half a dozen psalms along with a song by the kabbalist Shlomo Alkabetz (c. 1500–1576). The mystics introduced this service. Many think that the purpose of the service is to welcome the Sabbath, but this is not true. The word Shabbat is in the song Lecha Dodi, but it does not refer to the weekly Shabbat. It refers to the messianic age. Without explaining the song here in any detail, as I have done so elsewhere, I will just summarize that the song seeks the joining of two elements of the *sephirot* (spheres), which the mystics think will bring about the messianic age once they merge. Non-mystics ignore the original intent of the song and read into it the welcoming of the Shabbat and think how important the Shabbat is in their lives.

---

were added, the book became too large and unwieldy, so daily and Shabbat prayers were placed in a book called siddur and holiday prayers in one called machzor. *Siddur* means "arrangement," referring to the arrangement of the prayers, what is said and when. *Machzor* means "cycle," referring to the cyclical holidays throughout the year.

ANOTHER EXAMPLE

It is an Ashkenazic[2] tradition in many families to sing Psalm 126, Shir Hamaalot, before Birkat Hamazon, the blessings following the eating of a full meal, on Shabbat and joyous occasions such as festivals, weddings, circumcisions, and a pidyon haben.[3] Many scholars are convinced that the composition of this joyous psalm was when the Judeans returned to Judea after the Babylonian captivity in the sixth century BCE. The song speaks of the return: "When God returned the captives to Zion, it was like a dream."[4]

Jews loved *Shir Hama'alot* so much that many religious Zionists such as Rabbi Tzvi Yehuda Kook wanted to make it the national anthem of the State of Israel in 1948.

THE MYSTICAL EXPLANATION FOR ITS CHANTING AFTER EATING

The mystical book *Zohar* explains the practice.[5] It states that remembering the destruction of the temple after eating is fitting because prayers regarding the temple are as if one built the temple.[6]

HOW DO WE INTERPRET "AS IF ONE BUILT THE TEMPLE"?

Mystics believe in sympathetic magic. When the *Zohar* states "as if he built the temple," it most likely means he is magically contributing to the building of the temple.

Sir James George Frazer explained the phrase sympathetic magic in his justly famed book *The Golden Bough*, published in 1889. Frazer divided sympathetic magic into two kinds: that relying on similarity and that relying on contact or contagion. He wrote:

---

2. Ashkenazic Jews are from Germanic and other western European Christian countries. Sephardic Jews for the most part are from Muslim countries.
3. Some families add verses at the end from Psalms 145:21, 115:18, and 106:2.
4. Psalm 137 is sung instead of Psalm 126 on weekdays. It deals with the destruction of the temple and the sad beginning of the exile in 586 BCE, while Psalm 126 describes the happy end. It was felt that singing Psalm 137 on joyous occasions is inappropriate. Psalm 137 begins, "By the rivers of Babylon, we sat and remembered Zion."
5. Moses de León, *Zohar, Parashat Terumah* 157b.
6. See Rabbi Isaiah Horowitz, *Sheney Luchot Habrit* (NY: Lambda Publishers Inc., 2000) *Shaar Ha'otiyot qof* 170, where he echoed the teachings of the *Zohar*. Other mystics also did this.

> If we analyze the principles of thought on which magic is based, they will probably be found to resolve themselves into two: first, that like produces like, or that an effect resembles its cause; and, second, that things which have once been in contact with each other continue to act on each other at a distance after the physical contact has been severed. The former principle may be called the Law of Similarity, the latter the Law of Contact or Contagion. From the first of these principles, namely the Law of Similarity, the magician infers that he can produce any effect he desires merely by imitating it: from the second he infers that whatever he does to a material object will affect equally the person with whom the object was once in contact, whether it formed part of his body or not.

An example of sympathetic magic is the practice of American Indians to dance up and down on earth to cause rain the fall from heaven.

In essence, the *Zohar* is saying, if we sing about the restitution of the temple, it will cause the restitution to occur.

Although I haven't seen this idea expressed by anyone else, it seems to me that the two unique Sukkot practices – pouring water on the altar (which ceased with the destruction of the temple) and banging *aravot* (willow branches) on the ground, up and down (which is still performed in the *hoshanot* ceremony) – were instituted as sympathetic magic. The practices take place at the beginning of the fall season when the rainy season began in Israel when Jews wanted to assure that the rain would be plentiful, so they encouraged rain to fall by using sympathetic magic.

Other examples of sympathetic magic are the opening of the door for the prophet Elijah during the Passover Seder when Jews recall the ancient exodus from Egypt and pray for the coming of the messianic age. Tradition states that Elijah will reappear before the advent of the messianic age to announce it. In order to entice Elijah to come visit each home, someone opens the door where a cup of wine awaits him. If we welcome Elijah on earth, it will, as supposed, cause his appearance by sympathetic magic.

Similarly, the mystics developed the practice to turn around to the entrance of the synagogue at the end of their song Lecha Dodi when they sing about the coming of the Sabbath on Friday night. Why turn to welcome the Sabbath? As stated previously, mystics saw the weekly Sabbath as a symbol and foretaste of the messianic age. By turning to greet the Sabbath, they were greeting the messianic age, and by sympathetic magic, they were helping it to come.

So too by singing about the temple after eating, sympathetic magic will help in its rebuilding.

WHAT IS A RATIONAL NON-MYSTICAL EXPLANATION OF THE CHANTING OF SHIR HAMAALOT?

I suggest that we should understand that we sing Shir Hamaalot because of the lesson in the *Ethics of the Fathers* 3:3 and 4, which states that Jews whether alone or with others should speak of Torah during their meals. The rabbis also compared the dinner table to the altar in the temple. They were suggesting that this was a perfect time and place to remember Jewish history and ideals. Where others may deal with food in a gluttonous manner, Jews should recognize that food is a gift from God.

Since many Jews are unable to speak of Torah, Jewish tradition introduced a part of the Torah for them to use, Psalms 126 and 137, dealing with a significant part of Jewish history. Thus, rather than magic, the singing of Shir Hamaalot aids Jews in fulfilling the suggestion to speak of Torah during the meal, reminds Jews of their nation's history, the bad and good times, and hopefully encourages them not to rely on a miracle, but to work to bring about a messianic age for all humanity.

Chapter Thirteen

Relying on God's Help Can Result in Tragedy

Relying on prayer and divine help in daily life when problems arise, and not following the wise advice of Maimonides to use one's intelligence, study the laws of nature, and act according to these laws, laws created by God, can, and usually does result in tragedy to oneself, family, friends, and acquaintances.

EXAMPLES IN THE TORAH AND LITERATURE

In my book *The Tragedies of King David,* I showed how disasters that affected King David's life and the life of his family and nation during his entire life and even after his death, were caused by his making one mistake. The mistake was his adulterous relationship with Bat Sheba, which led to his murder of her husband and members of his military unit. This led to his son's rape of the son's half-sister, the murder of this son, rebellion by another son, the death of this beloved son, banishment, and other similar tragedies caused by his children. David suffered greatly because of these acts. I will now show how the great Greek dramatist Sophocles taught the same lesson in his famous Oedipus Cycle: *Oedipus Rex, Oedipus at Colonus,* and *Antigone.*[1]

1. Sophocles. *Theban Plays: Oedipus Rex, Oedipus at Colonus,* and *Antigone,* 406 BCE.

OEDIPUS REX (OEDIPUS THE KING)

Sophocles was one of the four great Greek playwrights whose works are extant today. The others are Aeschylus and Euripides, both of whom wrote tragedies like Sophocles, and the humorist Aristophanes who mocked the philosopher Socrates as a man whose head was in a cloud. Sophocles lived around 496 to around 406 BCE. He wrote over a hundred plays and was quite famous during his lifetime. Only seven of his plays are extant. The Oedipus Cycle with three plays is his most well-known series. Sigmund Freud drew his idea of an Oedipus complex from it, although it is not hinted at in the plays. The famed thinker Aristotle called *Oedipus Rex* the most perfect tragedy because, among other things, it depicts a man on top of the world brought low by a single act; Aristotle's definition of a tragedy.

In the first play, Oedipus is the king of Thebes. He is happily married with two daughters and two sons, and has a good relationship with his wife's brother Creon. His city suffers from a plague and the inhabitants want him to do something to remove it. He sends a messenger to an oracle who claims that a huge wrong was committed and that the gods will not remove the plague until the wrong is righted. Not knowing that he was the man who did the wrong, he gives orders to find the culprit, and either kill or banish him from the city.

A blind prophet, Teiresias, reluctantly discloses the truth, which is that Oedipus is the guilty person. He is the man who brought the plague to his city Thebes. His crime was that he unwittingly killed his father, the king of Thebes, married his mother, and had children by her. He did not know that he killed his father. He felt that an unknown man was attacking him, and killed his attacker without knowing his identity. Oedipus is shocked, blinds himself and bans himself from Thebes. When Oedipus's wife who is his mother hears the truth, she kills herself.

WHY WAS OEDIPUS PUNISHED?

Why was Oedipus punished for a deed he did without any evil intent and why should the entire populace of Thebes suffer for his deed? I addressed this question in detail in my book *The Tragedies of King David*. Sophocles does not address the question or answer it. Briefly stated, no one received a punishment. God was not involved. What happened was the result of natural law. Every deed has consequences, even innocent deeds, and the consequences can affect many other people, including one's family and community, as happens here. People need to understand this and be careful how they act. They need to use their intelligence, study the laws of nature, understand how nature works, and act accordingly.

Maimonides wrote in his *Guide of the Perplexed* 3:17 and 18 that it is not "through the interference of divine providence that a certain leaf falls [from a tree], nor do I hold that when a certain spider catches a certain fly, that this is the direct result of a special decree and will of God in that moment.... In all these cases the action is, according to my opinion, entirely due to chance, as taught by Aristotle.... The prophets even express their surprise that God should take notice of man, who is too little and too unimportant to be worthy of the attention of the Creator." Maimonides offers quotes from the prophetical books. He then explains that divine providence does not mean that God interferes with and changes the laws of nature. God created the laws of nature and people need to know and use them. "I hold that divine providence can only proceed from an intelligent being; therefore, it is related and closely connected with the intellect. [How much providence people receive will depend on their use of their intellect.] Every person has his share of divine providence in proportion to... the person's intellectual development.... Study this chapter as it ought to be studied; you will find in it all the fundamental principles of the law."

OEDIPUS AT COLONUS

Oedipus at Colonus is a continuation of *Oedipus Rex*. It is now twenty years later. Oedipus is very old and very weak. He is led about by his daughter Antigone because he is unable to move about unaided. She must help him and suffers thereby because of her father's deed of twenty years ago. Oedipus is at Colonus, a place named after a legendary horseman. The people at Colonus are not pleased to have the evil man in their midst and want him and his daughter to leave. Oedipus does not want to go. He feels he has suffered enough. He wants to die and be buried here. Fortunately, the king, Theseus, allows him to stay, and helps him later when his mother's brother Creon comes to take him back to Thebes where he will harm him.

Oedipus discovers that his two daughters love him and try to help him, but his two sons turned out to be evil and are about to engage in a war. His younger son is holding the throne of Thebes and his older son, wanting to be king, gathered an army of seven troops to attack Thebes. The turning of his sons into evil men would in all probability not have happened if Oedipus had been home and not in exile, another consequence of his killing his father, along with the suffering of his daughters who needed to be involved in trying to care for him, and the suicide of his wife/mother.

(Interestingly, Oedipus dies in a similar fashion to Elijah in II Kings 2. According to *Oedipus at Colonus*, scene VIII, Oedipus said goodbye to those from whom he wanted to take leave then went off with a single man [King Theseus]. "But in what manner Oedipus perished, no mortal men could tell but Theseus. It was not lightning, bearing its fire from Zeus that took him off; no hurricane was blowing. But some attendant from the train of heaven came for him; or else the underworld opened in love the unlit door of earth. For he was taken without lamentation, illness or suffering, indeed his end was wonderful if mortal's ever was." Later, when Oedipus' daughter Antigone wants to see his grave, Theseus tells her that Oedipus made him swear that he would never reveal his burial place.)

Aristotle praised this play and said that it can be enjoyed in reading it as by watching the performance in the theater.

ANTIGONE

Sophocles' *Antigone* is the final play of his *Oedipus Cycle*. It is, in my opinion, a chiasm to the first play *Oedipus Rex* because it has similarities in details to the first play, especially Creon causing deaths unwittingly, the prophesy to him by the same blind prophet of future horrors, and like Oedipus in the first play, Creon is brought low to utter despair, pleading for death.

In this play, we learn that the two brothers, Oedipus's two sons, killed each other in their battle and their uncle Creon became king. Creon orders the brother who was ruling Thebes at the time of his brother's attack buried with honors, and the attacking brother's body left in the open to rot as punishment. Antigone, like many citizens of Thebes, thinks this is wrong. She is caught trying to bury her brother, and Creon sentences her to death by placing her in an enclosure and starving her. Creon ignores the fact that Antigone is affianced to his son Haimon. Haimon pleads with his father to pardon Antigone and swears that if he fails to do so, he will not see him again. Creon does not back down.

As with Oedipus, the blind prophet Teiresias comes to King Creon and warns him that he has brought a new calamity upon himself and others. He is persuaded to release Antigone, but is too late. Antigone and Haimon have killed themselves so that they can be together in death (like the later Romeo and Juliet play). Also, when Creon's wife hears that her son Haimon is dead, she stabs herself and dies, as did Oedipus's wife/mother. Creon cries, "Let death come quickly.... I have been rash and foolish. I have killed my son and my wife." And the chorus chants, "There is no happiness where there is no wisdom." Acts have natural consequences that a wise person foresees.

Chapter Fourteen
Jewish and Christian Concepts of Repentance

Repentance as we know it today is not a biblical concept despite the thinking of many[1] that the prophet Hosea talked about it. Hosea 14:2 states "*Shuvah Yisrael ad Hashem Elokekha*" (Return Israel to the Lord your God). Actually, Hosea says in chapter 14 what he said several times in earlier chapters when he also used the word *shuvah* (return): stop worshiping idols, return and worship only God. It was only long after the lifetime of Hosea that Judaism developed the idea that one can repair wrongs that one committed by repentance.

WHAT IS TESHUVAH?

Neither the term teshuvah nor the concept of repentance as we know it today, the purging and expunging of misdeeds appear in the Torah. The ancients, Israelites and non-Israelites, believed that what one said, especially vows, or what one did is not erasable. When an egg is broken, its shards are unrepairable. They thought that the only remedies for misdeeds are by punishment.[2]

Scholars, as I explained in my earlier books, suppose that the current idea that people can nullify misdeeds by doing teshuvah developed in three stages.[3]

1. Including apparently Babylonian Talmud, *Yoma* 86a.
2. This concept is reflected in the Talmudic view that death atones. Babylonian Talmud, *Shabbat* 32a, *Yoma* 86a, *Sanhedrin* 43b and 47a–b.
3. *Olam Hatanakh, Devarim,* 221–23.

It began around 722 BCE. I wrote about the history of repentance in my earlier books, therefore I will not repeat the history here.[4] Instead, I will show that the current Jewish concept that one can repair wrongs by repentance, does not exist in Christianity.

The post-Hosea concept of repentance, teshuvah in Hebrew, dealing with common behavior, but not idol worship is a practical endeavor. Repentance doesn't magically absolve people of wrongs they committed. It's not abracadabra. Jewish repentance practices such as saying prayers and giving charity can only remind people to take practical measures to correct their behavior. It is a common mistake to think that Jews go to the synagogue during Rosh Hashanah and Yom Kippur to say prayers in the hope that God will wipe out any wrongs committed. Prayers do not do this. The purpose of the prayers is to prompt *us* to correct the wrongs we did in the past and change our future behavior. Change must come from the person.

Most people misunderstand repentance and confessions as they do the ancient sacrifices, as pseudo-magical recitations that remove misdeeds – as if words recited during a synagogue service could somehow change the past, erase the slap a husband gave his wife, and restore a loving relationship. "I don't understand why you're still angry," the husband wails. "I did teshuvah in the synagogue!" This isn't the way life works.

Maimonides put it this way:[5] teshuvah is when a person decides to abandon his or her past misdeeds, resolves not to do them again, thinks how to correct them, and develops habits to assure that they are not repeated. People do these four steps without the need of clergy, sacrifices, or even prayer.

Repentance requires the guilty person to act. It is not a state of mind, or words, or prayers, or the aid of another person. In the biblical book of Jonah, for example, it was not mind, words, prayers, or the aid of clerics, but the deeds of the people of Nineveh that caused God not to destroy their city as God had previously planned. "When God saw what they did, how they returned from their evil ways, God changed the evil that God had said would be done to them, and did not do it."

---

4. Drazin, *Mysteries of Judaism I* and Israel Drazin, *Unusual Bible Interpretations: Hosea* (Jerusalem: Gefen Publishing House, 2017).
5. Maimonides, *Mishneh Torah, Hilkhot Teshuvah.*

THE CHRISTIAN IDEA IS ENTIRELY DIFFERENT

Christianity changed the concept to give Jesus a mission, specifically to explain the crucifixion. It happened this way. Paul felt he had a mission to convert pagans to Judaism, for the early Christians were Jews who had some attachment to Jesus.[6] Paul taught the pagans that they could join the Jews without observing the Torah and such laws as circumcision and kashrut, laws the pagans disliked and that held them back from converting. Paul said that they could be "saved" by believing in Jesus, for Jesus died so that the wrongs of people would be erased and they could be saved.

If one denies Paul's idea that the only way that one can erase past misdeeds is through belief in Jesus, this would be saying there was no reason for Jesus's crucifixion. Thus, while Jews continued to believe that they could erase their wrong deeds through changing their behavior though repentance, Christianity began to believe that repentance could not nullify prior bad behaviors, only Jesus could do it for them, and one could approach Jesus through his clergy.

The biblical book Song of Songs is about the love between a man and a woman. Rabbi Akiva interpreted the story as an allegory describing the relationship between humans and God. Using this analogy, the Christian idea seems to be: one spouse (God) says to the other spouse (humans), "Do nothing about the wrong you committed and do not talk to me about it, go instead to a mediator [clergy] and request the mediator to nullify what you did; I gave mediators the power to nullify your wrongs."

---

6. There was no clear dogma in the early Christian era.

Chapter Fifteen
Deathbed Prayer/Confession

Many cultures advise their people that when dying they should say a prayer or confession. If they are not able to do so then they should have someone, preferably a member of the clergy, but if one is not available, then anyone, such as a family member or doctor, say this for them. If this hasn't been possible before the person passes away, then it should be done after death. Those who engage in this practice suppose that the recital will assure that heaven/God will hear the words and forget about all the wrongs the person committed while alive and give the individual rewards. Different religions have different ways of doing this. Catholics, for example, encourage people to confess to a priest who has authority to absolve the dying from their sins. The priests also say certain prayers, known as Last Rights and anoint the individual to remove the sins.

DEATHBED CONFESSION IN TALMUD

The Babylonian Talmud, *Shabbat* 32a reflects the view of many Jews who fear death or what occurs after death. It states, "Our rabbis taught: If one falls sick and his life is in danger, he is told, 'Make confession, for all who are sentenced to death make confession.'" In other words, just as criminals are told to confess before they are executed, so too all people who are about to die should do so as well. Significantly, this Talmudic statement does not say that the confession will whitewash away all misdeeds.

Ethics of the Fathers 2:10 states, "Repent one day before your death," which Babylonian Talmud, *Yoma* 153a explains, since a person does not know when death occurs, people should repent every day. The rabbis are not speaking here about a deathbed repentance, they are advising people to improve their behavior daily.[1]

DIFFICULTY

Since, as we saw, prayers and confessions do not produce magic and the purpose of prayer and confession is to encourage people to think about their past misdeeds, decide to change, and develop habits that aid a person to improve behavior, does the practice of deathbed confessions and prayers make sense?

THE TORAH

The Torah does not even hint that people should make confessions or say certain prayers on their deathbed. It appears that the practice arose during the Middle Ages.

THE ORIGIN OF SAYING THE SHEMA BEFORE DYING

The idea that developed among Jews to say the verse Shema, contained in Deuteronomy 6:4 – "Hear Israel, the Lord is our God. The Lord is one" – is an idea most likely prompted by two legends, both of which were misunderstood.

The first is Babylonian Talmud, *Pesachim* 56a, which tells the story:[2] "Rabbi Shimon the son of Lakish said, 'Jacob called his sons and said, "Gather and I will tell you." Jacob wanted to reveal to them when the end of days will occur, but the divine presence left him. Jacob wondered, "Perhaps [this happened because] there is imperfection amongst my offspring," as Abraham bore Ishmael and Isaac bore Esau. [So, too, my children may be idol worshippers]. Whereupon, his children responded, "Hear Israel, the Lord is our God, the Lord is one. The same way you have only one God in your heart, we have only one God in our hearts."'"

It is a mistake to think that Jacob recited the Shema on his deathbed as it was his children who did so. Also, this is only a legend.

The second tale upon which many rely to say Jews should recite the Shema on their deathbed is based on the story of Rabbi Akiva who was brutally murdered

---

1. Babylonian Talmud, *Yoma* 86b and other sources speak about the benefits of repentance but, again, they are speaking of improving one's life, not deathbed confessions.
2. The Midrash, *Deuteronomy Rabba* 2:35 has a slightly different version of the legend.

by the Romans around 165 CE. The story states that before dying Rabbi Akiva recited the Shema.[3] Many people think that since the sage Rabbi Akiva recited the Shema before dying, they should do so also. However, this is also a mistake. The story of Rabbi Akiva's death is only a legend; we do not know how he died. Secondly, even according to the legend, Rabbi Akiva recited the Shema because the time had arrived to say the Shema in the prayer service; meaning, he did not neglect saying the prayer service as the Romans killed him.

THE FIRST USAGE OF SAYING SHEMA BEFORE DYING

Rabbi Evan Hoffman of Congregation Anshe Shalom in New Rochelle, NY has a brilliant and learned weekly *Thoughts on the Parashah*. In his August 17, 2019 article he writes about Ivan Marcus's, "Performative Midrash in the Memory of Ashkenazi Martyrs," where he shows that the Jewish victims of the First Crusade in 1096 were first to recite Shema in connection with martyrdom. They were acting out the midrashic version of Rabbi Akiva's death. Nevertheless, Marcus noted that the practice initiated in Germany by the victims of 1096 did not catch on everywhere. There is no mention of the Shema in connection with various historical events. Some of these are the blood libel at Blois in 1171, the massacre of the Jews of York in 1190, or the murder of the wife and daughters of Rabbi Elazar ben Judah of Worms in 1196. Nor is the Shema mentioned in connection with the blood libel at Troyes in 1288, the Lepers and Shepherds Crusade of 1320, the pogrom against the Jews of Spain in 1391, or the persecution of the Jews of Portugal in 1497. More significantly, the saying of Shema in 1096 was not a deathbed confession. It was a declaration of persecuted martyrs by crusaders because they were Jewish. They recited the Shema as an affirmation that they were and would remain Jews who believed in the one God.

THE ORIGIN OF THE DEATHBED CONFESSION

Rabbi Hoffman tells us that the earliest rabbinic text calling upon even non-martyrs to make a deathbed profession of faith is *Sefer Toldot Adam v'Chava*, by Rabbenu Yerucham ben Meshulam (fourteenth century Spain). Rabbenu Yeru-

3. The legend is told in the Babylonian Talmud, *Berakhot* 61b and the Jerusalem Talmud, *Berakhot* 14b. The Shema is the centerpiece of the morning and evening Jewish prayer service.

cham cites a no longer extant passage from the works of Nachmanides urging a dying person to say, "The Lord God is true, His Torah is true, His prophet Moses is true, blessed is the Name of His glorious kingdom for all eternity." The ailing person is then to recite Psalm 145 followed by a heartfelt confession. Lastly, the dying person verbalizes his or her belief in the Maimonidean Principles of Faith including: the fact of God's existence; His uniqueness and oneness; His incorporeality; His chronological precedence; His worthiness to be worshipped; the existence of prophecy; the supremacy of Moses's prophecy and the giving of a heavenly Torah through Moses. Also that our current Torah is the same as the original Torah; that the Torah is not to be replaced with another revealed corpus; that God knows all of man's actions; that God rewards the righteous and punishes the wicked; that the Messiah will come and that the dead will be resurrected. Throughout the declaration, the dying person thinks about God and the Sinaitic Revelation.

The one verse most conspicuously missing from Rabbenu Yerucham's deathbed formula is Deuteronomy 6:4, the Shema. The great halakhic codifiers and commentators that followed Rabbenu Yerucham – Rosh, Tur, Karo,[4] Isserles, Levush, Bach, and Gra – all make no mention of the Shema as part of the deathbed liturgy.

Rabbi Hoffman tells us that Rabbi Abraham Danzig (1748–1820) appears to be the first halakhist to incorporate Shema into the deathbed rite. He cited Rabbenu Yerucham almost verbatim, but added this ending: "Hear O Israel, the Lord is our God, the Lord is One. Blessed is the Name of His glorious kingdom for all eternity."[5] Rabbi Hoffman suggests that Rabbi Danzig maybe codifying an existing popular practice. However, we have no way of ascertaining how old that practice was, whether the laity initiated the practice, or if rabbinical authorities originated it. Rabbi Hoffman adds that it is likely that the custom developed in East Central Europe in the eighteenth century.

SUMMARY

The deathbed recital of Shema is not biblical. It is an innovation in Judaism from the late Middle Ages. It is not a prayer nor a confession. It is an affirmation of

---

4. Joseph Karo's formula is in his *Shulchan Arukh Orach Chaim* 338:2.
5. Rabbi Avraham Danzig, *Chochmat Adam* 151:12.

religious identity. It allows the individual Jew, irrespective of how devoted the dying people were to practicing Judaism during their lifetime, to spend their final moments of life affirming a powerful feeling of solidarity with all Jews by reciting what Jews consider the basic teaching of Judaism, the acceptance of the divinity of God.

Chapter Sixteen
Does the Torah Mandate Saying Shema Twice Daily?

The rule that Jews should say the Shema twice daily is not a biblical command. It is a rabbinical enactment based upon Torah words.

WHAT DOES THE TORAH SAY?

Deuteronomy 6:4–9 states:

> Hear, Israel, the Lord is our God, the Lord is one. You shall love the Lord your God with all your heart and with all your soul and with all your might. And these words that I command you today shall be on your heart. (1) You shall teach them diligently to your children, (2) talk of them when you sit in your house, (3) when you walk by the way, (4) when you lie down and when you rise. (5) You shall bind them as a sign on your hand, and they shall be as frontlets between your eyes. (6) You shall write them on the doorposts of your house and on your gates.

By numbering the items in the paragraph, it should be clear that the six items are six ways in which "these words," meaning the words "You shall love the Lord your God with all your heart and with all your soul and with all your might… shall be on your heart."

"Heart" in the Torah means "mind" and "soul" in the Torah means "body." Scripture tells us that there are six ways to remind us of the command to love, that is think about God, which is in the second sentence of the paragraph.

You must (1) teach about God to your children. (2) You must talk about it at home as well as (3) when you leave your home. (4) You must talk about God all day, from when you get up in the morning until you go to sleep. (5) You must think of God when you work (hand) and when you think (frontlets between your eyes). (6) You should remember God whenever you leave your house or city.

THE PARAGRAPH DOES NOT SPEAK ABOUT RECITING THE SHEMA

First, the six items do not address the Shema sentence, but the sentence about loving God that follows it. Second. The purpose of all six delineated items is to keep the love, which is knowledge of God, constantly in mind (on your heart).

The rabbis invented the idea to say the Shema in the morning and evening services. Neither of these services are mentioned in the Torah and neither is said exactly when one lies down and when one rises.

SUMMARY

The practice of saying the Shema in the morning and evening services is of rabbinic origin. Although not biblically mandated, it is undoubtedly a very good practice because the Shema is a basic Jewish idea, the existence of God. It is the central part of these services with the other prayers built around it.

BEING MISLED BY BIBLICAL WRITING STYLES

Chapter Seventeen
The Bible Does Not Tell Us Everything

Many religious people of all religions accept the Five Books of Moses, the Torah, as a divine document. They see that the Torah has many stories, and are convinced that they understand the stories, which teach them lessons. The truth is different. While the Torah relates many events, it rarely explains them. Virtually all the biblical tales are obscure. In most instances, we do not even know what is happening and why it is happening. In many, we do not know who is involved.

AN INSUFFICIENTLY RECOGNIZED BIBLICAL STYLE

1. One of the first stories is creation. We learn that it occurred in six days and that God rested, ceased from work on the seventh day. Why did creation occur this way? Doesn't God have the power to create in a single day? Why have this version of how God created the world?
2. God creates a man and sees that the man is lonely. Why didn't God know this before man was created? Doesn't God have a superb intellect?
3. Cain and Abel are born. Cain works with animals while Abel works with vegetation. What is the reason for this information?
4. Cain kills Abel. We do not know why he did so, nor do we know why this story is important.
5. One of the most significant obscurities is the widely known verse in Deuteronomy 6:4, "Hear Israel, *Y-H-V-H* is our God: *Y-H-V-H* is one." What does "one" mean? We have no certain idea. We can only guess. Many, but not all, think it may mean unique, that God is better than every other thing, better

than the gods of other nations, or that God is very powerful, or that God is indivisible. The word or name *Y-H-V-H* is also obscure. Many, but not all think it is not a name like Joseph, but, as previously discussed, it is most likely, but not certainly, a description of God, that *Y-H-V-H* is based on a Hebrew word meaning "being," that it is stating that God is eternal, God was, is, and will be.

These are just a few of more than a hundred tales told without any explanation. Also:

1. Even biblical laws can be obscure. For example, the Sabbath is one of the most important commands of the Bible. It is one of God's first commands. It is in the Decalogue. Yet the commandment is unclear. When the Torah states that Jews are obligated to make it *kadosh*, usually translated "holy," how are we supposed to do that? Does *kadosh* mean "holy," and if so, what is "holy"? Alternatively, does it mean what some scholars say are, "distinct" and "different."
2. In the Exodus 20 version of the Decalogue, the word *shamor* ("keep" or "watch") is used, but in the Deuteronomy 5 version, it is *zachor* (remember). Are these two different commands? How does one "keep" and how does one "remember"? The Decalogue does not say.
3. The law about the place for sacrifices is another example. While we previously discussed Jerusalem, we can look now at the fact that the Torah is not explicit when it states the law. Deuteronomy 12:11 and close to two dozen other verses state that sacrifices may only be brought in the place that God will choose. Yet, despite the importance of this command, as indicated by the number of its repetitions, the Torah does not indicate what the place is that God will choose. In fact, for many generations, sacrifices were in locations outside of Jerusalem. It seems clear that there is no specificity so that the Israelites can make the decision themselves where to place the temple in Canaan, later called Israel.
4. There are two tales of Jacob being renamed Israel, (1) by the man with whom he wrestled in Genesis 32:29, and (2) by God in 35:10. Rashi and others explain that the man was not renaming Jacob, but that he was only foretelling that God changes his name in the future. Why was Jacob called by the name Jacob at times in the future and other times by the name Israel; if his name was changed, we would expect that he would be called only Israel. Many

traditional commentators explain that his name was not changed; he now had an additional name.

The following story also makes our point.

THE STORY OF MELCHIZEDEK

The strange tale of Melchizedek is in three sentences in Genesis 14:18–20. It is an anecdote about Abraham and Melchizedek. We will see that we do not know who Melchizedek is, what he and Abraham are doing, and why they are doing whatever they are doing.

The three sentences are in the middle of a report about a war engaged in by the patriarch Abraham. We learn that "five kings," apparently meaning the armies of five nations, including Sodom and Gomorrah, went to war against "four kings" (nations), and were defeated. The four took booty, including men and women, among whom was Lot, Abraham's nephew. When Abraham heard of the capture of his nephew, he gathered an army of 318 men and went to rescue him, beat the five kings, and returned home with his nephew and the booty.

> Then Melchizedek king of Salem brought bread and wine (to Abraham). He was the priest (Hebrew *kohen* the name/function given to Moses's brother Aaron and his descendants) of God Most High (Hebrew: *El Elyon*).
>
> He blessed him and said, "Blessed be Abram [Abraham's name before God changed it a later time] of God Most High, maker of heaven and earth.
>
> And blessed be God Most High who delivered your enemies into your hand." And he gave him a tenth of all (the booty).

The story ends with the king of Sodom asking Abraham, despite being defeated in the battle, to give him every captured human, but he agreed that Abraham could keep the rest of the booty. Abraham replied that he swore to "the Lord [Hebrew: *Y-H-V-H*], God Most High, maker of heaven and earth" that he would take no booty for himself from what is acquired from the battle.

OBSCURITIES IN THIS SHORT TALE

The most significant obscurities in this three-sentence story reveal that it is impossible to understand what transpired.

1. Who was Melchizedek?
2. Is Melchizedek a name, or a title like Pharaoh, is it a description such as "king of Zedek," "righteous king," or something else?
3. Where is Salem?
4. Why was he both the king and priest?
5. What was Melchizedek's function as priest (*kohen*)?
6. What was his involvement in the war?
7. Was it an unusual act to bring bread and wine?
8. What is the significance of the gift?
9. What is the meaning of *El Elyon*? Is this simply another name for *Y-H-V-H?* Note that Melchizedek describes *El Elyon* as the "maker of heaven and earth," an act that the Torah states God performed. Note also that Abraham equates *Y-H-V-H* with *El Elyon* maker of heaven and earth in his discussion with the king of Sodom.
10. What was the content of Melchizedek's blessing of Abraham; in other words, what did Melchizedek want God to give Abraham?
11. It is unclear who gave the gift of a tenth. Did Abraham hand Melchizedek a tenth of the booty despite saying to the king of Sodom that he gave up all rights to the booty? Moreover, if despite this he gave Melchizedek a tenth, why did he give him a gift and why a tenth and not another percentage? On the other hand, did Melchizedek give Abraham a gift of a tenth and, if so, a tenth of what and why did he do so?
12. Melchizedek called the deity *El Elyon* three times, once in each of the three verses. When Abraham replied to the king of Sodom when the king requested that he be given the humans that were taken as booty, Abraham said that he swore to "the Lord (Hebrew: *Y-H-V-H*), God Most High, maker of heaven and earth." Why did Abraham add *Y-H-V-H*? Why didn't Melchizedek add it? Should we understand that the addition has no significance, that both men were speaking about the same deity? Or, is Abraham correcting Melchizedek and saying that Melchizedek was referring to a pagan deity, but only *Y-H-V-H* is the God most high?
13. The Melchizedek story seems to be misplaced. Just before the three verses, in verse 17 that the king of Sodom went to meet Abraham. After the three verses about Melchizedek, verse 21 continues verse 17 by stating what the king said

to Abraham when he met him. Why place the Melchizedek tale in the middle of another account? This practice of inserting a story in the middle of another story and interrupting it is not unique. Genesis 38, for example, interrupts the story of Joseph and seems to have no connection to the story it is interrupting. Does the Melchizedek story have any connection to the battle of the four and five kings? If yes, how?

14. Melchizedek is also mentioned in Psalm 110:4 where the psalmist is apparently referring to King David or his descendants and says: "The Lord swore and will not relent: 'You are a priest forever like Melchizedek.'" What does this mean? Does it help clarify the three verses? Is it a prediction regarding the future as claimed by the New Testament?[1]
15. Why was this story included in the Torah? Does it teach us anything? Or, do the obscurities make us think? If the latter, think about what?

There is no certainty in answering these obscurities. Any suggested solution is pure speculation.

SOME SPECULATIONS WHICH ARE OBVIOUSLY NOT BASED ON FACTS

While evaluating the following we need to recall that Maimonides taught in his long essay called *Chelek* that people who think Midrashim are true are fools and those who dismiss them because they aren't true are also fools, because Midrashim were composed to teach lessons, proper behavior.

1. Rashi relying as usual on a Midrash, here *Genesis Rabba,* states that Lot's capture was because he foolishly settled in Sodom, which teaches people to be careful where they settle.
2. Melchizedek according the Rashi and Babylonian Talmud, *Nedarim* 32b was Shem, the son of Noah. This identification gives Melchizedek status because Shem was saved with his father and family from the destruction of the flood and must have been worthy of being saved. Shem is also the ancestor of Abraham and was possibly the origin of the term "Semite." Nevertheless, if Melchizedek was Shem, why didn't the Bible call him Shem?[2]

1. Hebrews 5:6–10, 6:20, and 7:1–21. There are other ancient references to Melchizedek.
2. Eight humans were saved in the flood: Noah, his three sons, and their four wives.

3. Psalm 76:3. Aramaic Targumim (translations of the Hebrew to Aramaic), and the Genesis Apocryphon identify Salem with Jerusalem.[3] Psalms reads, "In Salem also is set His tabernacle." This identification gives Jerusalem some status. Although captured by King David many years later from pagans, it was once a holy site, the home of Melchizedek.
4. Both *El* and *Elyon* are names of specific pagan deities, but while Melchizedek uses them, this does not necessarily indicate that he was referring to a pagan deity.[4] If we understand that *El Elyon* refers to *Y-H-V-H*, perhaps the tale is telling us that *Y-H-V-H* is the only true God Most High, despite some pagans referring to their idol by this title (Nachmanides).
5. God is described as *El Elyon* in four psalms – 7:18, 47:3, 57:3, and 78:56 – but there is no indication in the psalms that the name refers back to the Melchizedek story. Does the name/title in Psalms mean something different from that in Genesis?
6. Bread and wine symbolized the sacrifices brought (in the temple in Jerusalem) by the descendants of Shem and Abraham (Rashi and *Genesis Rabba*). Actually, the main ingredient of the sacrifices was the meat.
7. Rashi suggests that Abraham was the one who gave the tenth to Melchizedek because Melchizedek was a priest. He does not address the issues of the law of giving a share of produce, promulgated centuries later during the time of Moses, and even then, Levites, not priests got a tenth and priests received less than this amount.[5]
8. Yehuda Kiel quotes a source in his *Commentary to Sefer Bereishit*[6] that blessing here means extoled, not a prayer; Melchizedek was recognizing that Abraham was beloved by God.

SUMMARY

One should not imagine that I am criticizing the Torah by insisting that much in it is obscure. The opposite is true. Despite what most people would imagine.

3. Nahman Avigad and Yigal Yadin, *A Genesis Apocryphon: A Scroll from the Wilderness of Judaea* (Jerusalem: Magnes Press, Hebrew University, 1956).
4. E.A. Speiser, *The Anchor Bible: Genesis* (Doubleday, 1964).
5. Numbers 18:21.
6. Yehuda Kiel, *Sefer Daat Mikra: Bereishit* (Jerusalem: Mossad Harav Kook, 1997).

Jorge Borges was right when he wrote that all good literature must have ambiguity and obscurity. He added that this results in two authors of good literature: the one who wrote it and the one who reads it and interprets the ambiguities and obscurities. "A book is more than a verbal structure or series of verbal structures; it is the dialogue it establishes with its reader and the intonation it imposes upon his voice and the changing and durable images it leaves in his memory. A book is not an isolated being: it is a relationship, an axis of innumerable relationships."[7] Obscurities give us an opportunity to read our own ideas into what the author states, and build upon it, and broaden and deepen our thinking.

The story of Melchizedek is an example of the many biblical tales that sound interesting, but virtually everything about them is incomprehensible. All we can say about these tales are that they were composed to make us think, to add to the tales our own ideas, and use them to improve our understanding of life and what is required of us.

Not only is there value by telling the tales in a somewhat obscure manner, the same applies to the laws. Leaving out details makes it possible for generations after the revelation of the Torah to add and to change what was suitable for the generation of the revelation.

---

7. Unfortunately, I read Borges' insight many decades ago and I am unable to find where he wrote it. Be this as it may, the idea is certainly correct.

Chapter Eighteen
What Happened to Bethuel?

The story of Abraham's servant's encounter with Rebekah's family is another example of obscurities. One of several is where was her father Bethuel?

DID ABRAHAM'S SERVANT MEET REBEKAH'S FATHER?

Abraham sent his trusted servant to his kindred in his former country to take a wife for his son Isaac.[1] The servant met Rebekah and decided that she would be the perfect wife for Isaac. He gave her jewelry. She "ran and told her mother's house" what transpired.[2] Her brother Laban ran, met the servant and negotiated the betrothal.[3] Then surprisingly, later in verse 50, Laban and Bethuel, Rebekah's father, told the servant that if Rebekah wanted to go, she could go.

Why did Rebekah run to her mother's house? Why not to the house of her parents or her father's house? Why is her brother Laban doing the negotiations? Where was her father? Why does he suddenly appear in verse 50 giving his consent when not previously mentioned? All of these events are obscure.

Saadiah Gaon (882–942) and Rashi suggest that Rebekah wanted to show her new jewels to her mother for women appreciate jewelry more than men do. They also suggest that the women in this household had a separate dwelling where they worked. While not in Scripture, it is one possible explanation.

---

1. We do not know why both Abraham with Isaac and later Rebekah with Jacob wanted their son to marry within the family and why this practice was not continued with Jacob's children. Also, Rebekah did not like it that her son Esau married a Canaanite woman but her grandchildren did not have either of these scruples. Both items are obscure.
2. Genesis 24:28.
3. Genesis 24:29–49.

Where was Bethuel during the negotiations and why is he mentioned in verse 50?

As often happens, Midrashim attempt to answer obscurities. They generally suggest imaginative ideas that are clever but not suggested or implied in the biblical text, as happens here.

Midrash Genesis Rabba on the verse states that God killed Bethuel during the negotiations to protect Abraham's servant. The Midrash says Bethuel planned to kill the servant and steal the jewels he had with him.

Midrashic *Da'at Zekeinim Miba'alei Hatosafot* is similar. It also states that God killed Rebekah's father but give a more elaborate reason. Bethuel was the chief of the local clan and had the right to have sex with all women who were about to be married. He would do so before the wedding ceremony. He was such a crude person that he even wanted to bed his own daughter who during the negotiations with the servant became engaged to Isaac. God killed him lest Isaac get a non-virgin bride.

Readers may dislike the midrashic suggestions because while they may be entertaining, they are not in Scripture. Additionally, they conflict with the timeline. The problem with the biblical text is why was Bethuel's son negotiating the engagement without any mention of Rebekah's father, but he then inexplicably appears at the end of the negotiations agreeing that she can leave. Was he dead during the negotiations? Why is he alive at the end of the talks in verse 50 and approving her leaving to marry Isaac? Also, why is his name mentioned after the mention of his son's name in verse 50? Since he was Rebekah's and Laban's father, he should have been mentioned first.

Unable to find a satisfactory explanation of the obscurity, some scholars assert that this is a scribal error.[4] Some person placed Bethuel's name in verse 50 by mistake. He probably died of natural causes before the arrival of Abraham's servant, and was therefore not involved at all in the engagement negotiations. This would also explain why Rebekah ran to her mother's house – her father was dead – and why Laban discussed the matter with the servant.

---

4. Speiser, *The Anchor Bible: Genesis.*

Chapter Nineteen
Does the Torah Speak in Divine Language?

Abraham ibn Ezra (c. 1089–c. 1164) discusses two ideas in his commentary to the Decalogue in Exodus 20 where he considers the many differences in wording of the Exodus version from the Deuteronomy 5 version. They are: (1) The methodologies of Rabbi Akiva and Rabbi Ishmael, he does not identify the authors by name, but a full discussion of the views can be found in *Torah min Ha-Shamayim Be-Aspaḳlaryah shel Ha-Dorot* by Abraham Joshua Heschel (1907–1972). (2) Whenever an event is repeated in the Bible, the Torah adds something to the repetition that helps clarify the former version. The following is a discussion of the first item,

RABBI AKIVA VS. RABBI ISHMAEL

In the classic *Torah min Ha-Shamayim Be-Aspaḳlaryah shel Ha-Dorot* Abraham Joshua Heschel skillfully tells the methodology of Rabbi Akiva and the difference between him and Rabbi Ishmael. Gordon Tucker translated the work into English as *Heavenly Torah: As Refracted Through the Generations*. The two Talmudic sages lived around 130 CE and disagreed on how to interpret the Bible. Rabbi Akiva won out, and Rashi, Nachmanides, and most ancient Bible commentators as well as most Midrashim follow his view. Others, such as Rashi's grandson Rashbam, ibn Ezra, and Maimonides interpret the Torah as Rabbi Ishmael.

RABBI AKIVA'S BELIEF

Rabbi Akiva felt that the Bible is a word-for-word revelation from God. Since

God is perfect, is able to say concisely exactly what is meant to be said, and would never place any superfluous or non-relevant material in the divine book, whenever an idea is repeated in the Bible or there is an unusual word or change in spelling, God must have placed it to teach a lesson. People need to spot these additions and changes, and figure out what God meant to teach by placing them in the Bible.

The Akivian methodology goes so far as to even interpret the word *et*, which has no meaning in biblical Hebrew and is used in the Torah as a sign of the accusative. Under the Akivian method, when *et* appears it is suggesting not only what is mentioned, but also anything that can be associated with it. For example, when Genesis 1:1 states that God created *et hashamayim v'et haaretz*, the heaven and the earth, it should be understood that God created the heaven and earth and all that they contain. The methodology is also used for seeing rabbinic Midrash in the crowns on the biblical letters in the Torah scrolls used in synagogue services.[1]

RABBI ISHMAEL'S OPINION

Rabbi Ishmael disagreed. He felt that "the Torah [which is intended for humans] speaks in human language." For example, just as people repeat themselves for emphasis, to gain attention, for the sake of clarity, or to make their statement more flowery or poetic, so too does the Torah. Nothing should be read into repetitions, of which there are many. If God meant to teach an additional lesson, He wouldn't have hidden it in a repetition that doesn't mean or even imply what people read into it; God would have made an explicit statement.

RABBI AKIVA'S METHODOLOGY BECAME THE ACCEPTED WAY TO UNDERSTAND THE TORAH

Rabbi Akiva's students compiled the Midrashim and influenced most of the Talmudic rabbis, and later Bible and Talmud commentators such as Rashi, who based their teachings on Rabbi Akiva's method. Most rabbinical sermons today drawn from these sources are based on his method. Readers and listeners need to know that what they are reading, or what the synagogue rabbi is sermonizing, is based on what the commentator or rabbi thought (erroneously according to Rabbi Ishmael) was an unnecessary repetition or an unusual spelling.

---

1. Babylonian Talmud, *Menahot* 29b.

EXAMPLES

Most Judaic teachings including rabbinical laws and the imaginative midrashic versions of what transpired in biblical times hang from a flimsy string attached to the Akivian notion.

The following are examples from Genesis 23 and a couple of other passages where Rashi, the French commentator on Bible and Talmud, draws from the Torah text imaginative information that usually comprises non-sequiturs not hinted at in the text.

1. Genesis 9:10 repeats that God will establish his covenant in Noah's post-flood generation with humans and animals "all that goes out of the ark, every living thing of the earth." Rashi, following the methodology of Rabbi Akiva, wonders why the Torah adds "every living thing of the earth," when it already said that God made the covenant with "all that go out of the ark." He answers: the latter refers to demons, which were also included in the covenant. (Rashi was not alone in believing in the existence of demons. There are over three dozen discussions of demons in the Talmud. However, there is no explicit mention of demons in the Pentateuch.)
2. In Genesis 23:1, the Torah unnecessarily, according to Rashi, repeats years three times, "The life of Sarah [Abraham's wife] was a hundred years, and twenty years, and seven years." Rashi states that the repetition reveals that at 100 she was like 20 concerning sin, and at 20 she was as beautiful as a girl of seven. (The repetition of years, as in this verse, is characteristic biblical phraseology, and has no hidden meaning. It is in Genesis 5:5, 6, 7, 8, 10, 11, 23, 26: Exodus 12:40, 41, 25:10, and many other passages. None of them with the connotation that Rashi sees here.)
3. Again in 23:1, after mentioning that Sarah lived 127 years, Scripture repeats, "these are the years of Sarah's life." Why were these words added? Rashi says they inform readers that despite difficulties that Sarah had in her life, she felt that they were all good.
4. When Abraham negotiates with Ephron to purchase burial ground for his deceased wife Sarah, the Bible states in 23:10 that Ephron was sitting among the children of Heth. Rashi notes that the Hebrew word for "sitting" has an unusual spelling; it is missing the letter *vav*. He writes that the letter was

omitted to inform readers that "on that day he [Ephron] was appointed ruler over them [the children of Heth]. He was elevated [apparently Rashi means by God] because Abraham needed the elevated rank [to be able to negotiate with the leaders of the children of Heth]."

5. Why state both "created" and "made"? Genesis 2:3 seems to have a duplication, "which God created, had made." Ignoring the Ishmael idea that this is common human speech, ibn Ezra states that "had made" means that God gave the items the power to reproduce. Rashi's view is that duplication suggests that God did double work on the sixth day. Nachmanides understands "had made" as suggesting, "That which God had made out of nothing."
6. Rashi ignores the fact that there are hundreds of different spellings in the Torah. For example, there are differences in spellings in the Decalogue (Ten Commandments) of Exodus 20 and Deuteronomy 5. Even Ephron's name omits a *vav* in 23:16, not only 23:10. There Rashi says the Torah omits the *vav* to inform readers that Ephron diminished himself in how he handled his negotiations with Abraham. (Thus, inconsistently, in example 4 the missing *vav* is said to elevate and in example 5 to diminish.)
7. Rashi also interpreted the Torah by using gematriot. A gematria (the singular form of the word) is the numerical value of letters that make up words using the numerical value of each letter. The first letter of the Hebrew alphabet, an *aleph*, equals one, the second, a *bet*, two, and so on. Commenting on 24:1, Rashi is bothered by the Bible's need to tell readers that God blessed Abraham "with everything"; haven't we seen many instances of God's blessing to Abraham before? Why did God repeat this information? The Hebrew word for "with everything" is *bakol*. Rashi notes that the numerical value of the Hebrew letters of *bakol* is 52, the very same number as the Hebrew word *ben*, son. He writes that the Torah is stating that God blessed Abraham with a son, and then narrates how Abraham tried to secure a wife for this son. (The twelfth century rational sage Abraham ibn Ezra sarcastically commented, "God does not speak in gematriot.")

Chapter Twenty
Does the Bible Speak Mystically?

In addition to previously mentioned commentators, Nachmanides offers another example. Two of his methods are (1) to read the text literally even when what is stated is impossible and considered a parable or vision by Maimonides, and (2) to insist that the Torah is written in a kind of code; those who understand kabbalah will be able to see that the Torah is filled with mysticism.

NACHMANIDES AND MYSTICISM

As a mystic, Nachmanides, or using the Hebrew acronym Ramban (1194–1270), was the first person to introduce the idea that the Torah contains mystical notions, and the first to offer a mystical interpretation of the Bible. He was also the first to state that the Aramaic translation of the Pentateuch, Targum Onkelos, contains imaginative aggadic material and mysticism. It was as if he were arguing that if the Torah were true and mysticism is true, and Targum Onkelos is true, then it follows that the Torah and Targum Onkelos must contain mysticism.[1]

NACHMANIDES AVOIDS THE PLAIN MEANING OF SCRIPTURE

Unlike Maimonides's parabolic approach to the Book of Genesis, Nachmanides takes the opposite position and insists that what the Bible says actually happened. He insists that the Torah speaks about a real Garden of Eden and that Adam's dis-

1. See Israel Drazin, *Nachmanides: An Unusual Thinker* (Jerusalem: Gefen Publishing House, 2017) where I discuss his view with a refutation of it.

obedience was a historical event. Eden, he claims, occupies a place in the ancient Near East. The Edenic serpent was not a mythical character or a psychological symbol; it actually walked and talked.

In contrast, Maimonides explains in his *Guide of the Perplexed* 1:2 that the story has a significant allegorical meaning.

Similarly, later on in the Pentateuch, when Balaam's donkey spoke to the pagan prophet, Nachmanides maintains that the story means exactly what it says – the donkey talked. Once again, Maimonides explained that the event did not happen. Balaam, frightened by the task the king wanted him to do, imagined the event. His conversation with the donkey was the conversation he had with himself, his more rational self, warning him to be careful.

NACHMANIDES AND PROPHECY

Nachmanides's insistence that the Torah must be understood literally led him to disagree with Maimonides who did not think that prophecy was a communication from God, but rather the thinking of a man or woman of a higher than average intelligence who felt the need to communicate his or her understanding to the general public.[2]

Thus, for example, Maimonides understood that the story of the three strangers who visited Abraham was, as with Balaam, an internal discussion that Abraham had with himself. Nachmanides argued to the contrary that Abraham entertained real guests who were celestial angels, not figments of his imagination.

NACHMANIDES APPLIED HIS THINKING TO MANY EVENTS

He considered biblical unnatural events like speaking animals as actual occurrences, and regarded all the midrashic stories mentioned in rabbinic tradition as having occurred.[3]

He also believed in demons and sorcery since the Torah mentions that the Israelites should not consult them. He asserts that anyone who does not believe in demonic beings suffers from a heretical attitude toward the world. According

2. Maimonides, *Guide of the Perplexed* 2:32–48.
3. Drazin, *Nachmanides: An Unusual Thinker.*

to Nachmanides, if you believe in miracles, then you ought to believe demonic beings exist as well. He wrote:

> It is from this standpoint that you can come to realize the ruthlessness and stubbornness of the principal Greek Philosopher Aristotle – may his name be erased from memory – who denies the truth of many things which we have seen and has been publicized throughout the world. In Mosaic times, these truths were known to all for the wisdom of that generation pertained to spiritual matters, e.g., entities involving the demonic and sorcery. However, when the Greeks arose, Aristotle believed only in what the physical sciences could confirm. In his effort to establish the scientific disciplines, he denied the realm of the spiritual. Aristotle denied the existence of demons and all magical acts. For him, the world operated solely by natural law. But it is well-known and shown that this is not the case at all.[4]

Maimonides considered such a perspective to be superstitious nonsense.

4. Maimonides, "Torat Hashem Temimah," in *Kitvei Ha-Rambam*, ed. Charles Ber Chavel (Jerusalem: Mossad Harav Kook, 1963), vol. I, 147, 149.

Chapter Twenty-One
The Bible Repeats Itself

Here is Abraham ibn Ezra's second commentary to the Decalogue in Exodus 20, "Whenever an event is repeated in the Bible, the Torah adds something to the repetition that helps clarify the former version."

ANOTHER INTERPRETIVE METHOD NOTED BY IBN EZRA

Commenting upon the differences between the wording of the Decalogue in Exodus 20 and Deuteronomy 5, ibn Ezra explains, as previously stated, that whenever an event repeats in the Torah, additions are inserted in the repetition to clarify what was said previously.

EXAMPLES

When Moses retold the history of the Israelites to them in Deuteronomy, including the Decalogue, he changed the words formerly used in Exodus and added words to help the Israelites understand what he was saying.

Another example of this is the story of Abraham in Genesis 24 sending his servant to Aram-naharaim to bring back a woman who would become the wife of his son Isaac. Details of the conversation between Abraham and his servant are in the beginning of the chapter. Later, when the servant tells Abraham's family in Aram-naharaim about his mission, there are additional facts. It is a mistake to think that the servant added untrue facts when he told about his conversation with Abraham. This is simply the biblical narrative style – adding details in the retelling of the story.

In Genesis 27:4, Isaac requests his son Esau to hunt and bring him food "so that I could give you my blessing before I die." When his wife Rebekah told her son Jacob what she overheard, she added the words "before the Lord" – "that I would bless you before the Lord before I die." The addition may be what Isaac said or she added the words to impress her son whom she was trying to persuade to lie to his father about the importance of the blessing.

Chapter Twenty-Two
More than a Single Version of an Event

There are many instances in the Hebrew Bible where there are two accounts given of an event and the two differ from each other. The apparent disagreements exist in many biblical books, including the Five Books of Moses as noted by both ancient rabbis and modern scholars. Each took various approaches in explaining them. In regard to the book of Joshua, for example, critical scholars concluded that the differences show that more than a single author, perhaps as many as four, wrote the early drafts of Joshua and then they were assembled by an editor who, not realizing the book would later be canonized, chose not to resolve them. The rabbis suggested solutions for each apparent conflict. Frequently they asserted that two conflicting statements were describing the same event, but from a different perspective, and argued that both accounts were true – for example, when the book of Joshua states in one verse that Joshua set an ambush of five thousand and in another verse that he set an ambush of thirty thousand, these were two separate ambushes. Joshua set one ambush of five thousand and one of thirty thousand.

SOME EXAMPLES OF DUAL VERSIONS

1. Genesis 1 and 2 seem to have conflicting versions of the creation of humans. Genesis 1 states that God created a man and a woman, seemingly both at the same time, while Genesis 2 reports that the creation of Eve was later when Adam was lonely.
2. Genesis appears to have two versions regarding the creation of birds. Chapter

1 states that they emerged from water, while 2:19 states that God formed them from the ground.

3. God tells Noah in Genesis 6:19 to take two of every animal in the ark, a male and a female, but in 7:2–3 God directs him to take seven of all the clean animals.
4. Genesis 7:21–23 states that every being, humans and animals who breathe died in the flood. Yet, it appears that the race of giants, mentioned in 6:4, survived in the days of Moses in Numbers 13:33.
5. There are different accounts of the length of the Israelites enslavement Egypt. Genesis 15: 13–16 states 400 years, while Exodus 12:40 has 430. The rabbinical calculation is midrashic based on the numerical value of the Hebrew word *redu,* which equals 210 years.
6. In Genesis 24, for example, one version of Abraham's servant's trip to secure a wife for Isaac is told as it actually occurred, while the second version relates it from the servant's perspective.
7. In Genesis 32:29, a stranger renames Jacob Israel, but in 35:10, God gives him the new name.
8. Exodus 20 quotes the Decalogue revealed by God, while Deuteronomy 5's version is the same Decalogue from Moses's perspective.
9. There are two versions of how David met King Saul in Samuel 16 and 17. In 16, he is a member of King Saul's army. In 17, he is a simple shepherd.

EXAMPLES FROM A SINGLE BIBLICAL BOOK

In my book *Unusual Interpretations: Joshua,* I showed what appear to be many internal conflicts, two contrasting versions of a single event, all of these doublets occurred in this single book.

1. In chapter 4, one version has a monument set in the middle of the Jordan River, while a second version places it near the river.
2. Chapter 8, as previously stated, mentions that Joshua arranged an ambush of thirty thousand Israelites, but a second version has five thousand.
3. In chapter 9, the Gibeonites deal with the tribal leaders in one version and with Joshua in another.
4. Chapter 10 declares that all Canaanites in the locality were killed, however subsequent chapters disclose that some Canaanites escaped.

5. Chapter 11 narrates that Joshua vanquished Hebron during the seven years of occupation, but Caleb does so in chapter 14 after the seven-year period.
6. In chapter 14, Joshua gave Caleb the city of Hebron, but in 21:12, Joshua assigned it to the Levites.
7. The book has sentences saying that Joshua triumphed over all of Canaan, while others reveal that he was not successful.
8. Some statements in Joshua also differ with those in the book of Judges. According to Joshua, Israel took Canaanite territory in battles, but in Judges 1 and 2, the campaigns were engagements by individual tribes who seized their own territories.
9. In Joshua 12 Joshua conquered Megiddo, but Judges 1:27 reveals that the city was uncaptured.

SUMMARY

The talmudic rabbis noted these apparent differences and offered reasonable explanations as to why they say what they say. The apparent difference between the number of animals that Noah should take in the ark is a good example. It is the biblical style to make a general statement and later elaborate upon it giving details. The Bible tells us first in a general way that most of the animals taken were pairs. Later, when it gives details, it states to take seven "clean animals." It is clear that the increased number is because they are "clean," most likely meaning suitable as sacrifices.

Chapter Twenty-Three

The Use of Three, Another Biblical Style

As in fairy tales, the Bible uses the number three frequently. It does so 430 times in the Tanakh by simply mentioning the number of a multiple of it. The basic three-letter-root, *sh-l-sh,* appears 172 times, and the Hebrew form of three with the letter *hay* at its end appears an additional 258 times. There are also many multiples of three, such as thirty, which is in Scripture 172 times. Additionally, many events include three in some way, like events described three times. The numbers seven and ten also appear frequently. Ten is the result of combining the numbers three and seven.

AN EXAMPLE

The 139 verses in I and II Kings relating to Elijah serve as an example.

In I Kings 17, the number three appears twice; when Elijah stretches over the child, and when he cries to God, each three times. Twice it mentions three events in the chapter: the drought, the feeding by ravens, and the feeding by a widow; and the three times he made requests for food and drink from the widow; first just water, second for bread in order that he be fed first, and third that she bake again for herself and her son.

In chapter 18, the number three occurs when the chapter mentions that the events happened three years after the former events, and when Elijah poured water on the altar three times. There are five events in the chapter associated with the number three which I identified in my commentary.

In chapter 19, the number does not appear, but ten events associated with the number three are in the chapter, and listed in the commentary.

In II Kings 2, the number is mentioned only once when the sons of the prophets searched for three days. Four events also happen in threes.

The frequent use of the number three shows that the author used the number intentionally. Why did he do so? Three is also a number frequently used in fairy tales and in many other biblical books. Should we suppose that the biblical author is telling us that his history is not true, or that it is true but not precisely as told?

ARISTOTLE, IBN EZRA, AND HIRSCH

Aristotle considered three the perfect number by having a beginning, middle, and end, and said it indicates completeness. Judaism uses seven to signify completeness in various ways over a hundred times. Samson Raphael Hirsch, seeing seven as a sign of completeness, explains that circumcision occurs on the eighth day as a new beginning. Seven reminds Jews that God created the world from nothing or from preexisting matter, ceased creation on the seventh day (or period), and gave Jews laws to help them improve themselves and society. Abraham ibn Ezra said that while seven shows that something is complete, three, being about half of seven, implies an almost complete, or a long item. We do not know why Jews and non-Jews use the number three. Perhaps, it is because three items are easy to remember.[1] Sociologists tell us that phone companies restrict the telephone numbers to seven digits because most people cannot remember more than seven items.

MORE EXAMPLES

1. There are three patriarchs: Abraham, Isaac, and Jacob.
2. God made a covenant with the Israelites at Mount Sinai and asked them to agree, which they did three times, in Exodus 19:8, 24:3 and 7.
3. When Abraham went to sacrifice Isaac in Genesis 22, he went on a three-day journey.

---

1. For many mystically minded people, three has magic power. To accomplish something, one needs to do or say something three times. Joseph Karo, for example, was convinced that demons attach themselves to human bodies, especially their hands, while the individual sleeps. He wrote in his code of Jewish law, *Shulchan Arukh*, that the first thing people should do when waking is to wash their hands three times to rid themselves of demons.

4. The Israelites had to prepare for the revelation of the Decalogue in Exodus 19 for three days.
5. There are three kinds of misdeeds: *chet, pesha,* and *avon.*[2]
6. Adam and Eve had three sons mentioned in the Torah.
7. Noah and his wife had three sons.
8. Three angels visited Abraham and told him that he and Sarah would have a son in a year.
9. Abraham prepared a meal for them including three measures of fine meal.
10. The story of Melchizedek told in Genesis 14:18–20 is in three verses.
11. Melchizedek calls God *El Elyon* three times.
12. Hebrew words generally have a three-letter root.
13. There are three pilgrimage festivals, Passover, Shavuot, and Sukkot.
14. Moses set aside three cities in Trans-Jordan in Numbers 4:41.
15. Leah had 33 descendants in Genesis 46:15.
16. Genesis 5:22 mentions three hundred years of Enoch's life.
17. The length of Noah's ark was 300 cubits.
18. Only 300 men seemed worthy to join Gideon in Judges 6:9.
19. People rebelled against their oppressors in the 13th year in Genesis 14:4.
20. Three months after he had sex, Judah learned that the woman was pregnant in Genesis 38:24.
21. The High Priest thrice pronounced the Ineffable Name of God during his series of confessionals on *Yom Hakippurim* (Mishnah *Yoma* 6:2).
22. One recites the prayer Kol Nidrei three times on the eve of Yom Kippur.
23. The prayer "Blessed be the name of His glorious kingdom forever and ever" is recited three times at the end of Yom Kippur. (Contrary to what many think, Yom Hakippurim and Yom Kippur are two distinct holidays, as I explain in *Mysteries of Judaism 1*).
24. On holidays, one recites the thirteen attributes of God three times when removing the Torah from the ark to read.
25. The prayer *va'ani tephilati,* for salvation repeats three times after the recital of the thirteen attributes.
26. Rabbi Joseph Karo mandated in his *Shulchan Arukh* that people wash their

2. See "Greeks, like Jews, Did Not Have the concept of "Sin"' in chapter 35.

hands three times in the morning to wash away the demons that attack people during the night. (In contrast, people wash only twice before eating bread.)

27. In I Samuel 1, Channah calls herself a "maidservant" three times in her plea to God to give her a son.
28. Deuteronomy 28 repeats "the *sheger* of your herd and the *ashtaroth* of your flock" three times. *Sheger* and *Ashtaroth* were names given to a West Semitic goddess of fertility. Later, the words lost their original pagan meaning and came to mean "offspring" of livestock.
29. The word *kadosh* (holy), applicable to God, is said three times one after the other in the Kedusha prayer, during the repetition of the Amidah.
30. Tradition states that Abraham returned to health on the third day after his circumcision.
31. In II Samuel 9 *chesed*, indicating acts of loving kindness is repeated three times to highlight that this is the theme of the chapter.
32. As in many other cultures, three indicates a pattern. In Jewish law, living in a place for three years without any adverse claim creates a *chazakah*, an indication of ownership.
33. If three men, and according to many Orthodox three women, sit together at a meal and no man is present, one of the group can lead the grace after the meal with introductory words called *mezuman*.

Chapter Twenty-Four
Hyperbole, Another Ubiquitous Biblical Style

Most readers of the Bible fail to recognize that the Bible generally exaggerates. It most likely does so to highlight a point. However, readers need to be careful and not take such statements literally.

SOME EXAMPLES

1. Moses frequently speaks to all of the people. Even if we reduce the biblical number of Israelites who exited Egypt from the over 600,000 males of military age together with younger and older men, women, and children, as well as non-Israelites who the Bible states accompanied them, to even as low as several thousand, Moses could not speak loud enough for all to hear him. This frequent statement is hyperbole and likely made to stress that when Moses communicated a law or direction to tribal leaders, he made sure that the people would know what he said.
2. In Joshua 11:23, the Bible tells us that Joshua conquered all of Canaan. This is an exaggeration. He led the Israelites to conquer lots of land, but far from all of it. Indeed, the Israelites had difficulty with the many Canaanites who remained in the land for many generations. The Torah is overstating his accomplishments to give him credit for what he achieved.
3. Judges 21:11–12 describes an Israelite civil war in which the victorious tribes killed "every male and every woman that had lain with a man" and only virgins

remained alive. The Bible commentator Arnold Ehrlich states that this is most likely an exaggeration.

4. The prophet orders in Samuel 7:5 "assemble all Israel," but it means that tribal leaders or military men should come to him.
5. In Samuel 7:11 the "men of Israel" pursued the Philistines, but only the soldiers did so.
6. Samuel 8:4 relates that "all the elders" came to Samuel to complain, but it is unlikely that every elder came.

Chapter Twenty-Five
Similar Stories

Many biblical stories are understandable when comparing them with each other, seeing how the people involved act with each other, asking why an episode occurs, and observing how the stories are the same, or noting their differences.

EXAMPLES

1. There are striking similarities between Abraham's agreement to banish his son Ishmael from his home as demanded by his wife Sarah, which God confirmed, and his willingness to sacrifice his other son Isaac when God told him again to obey. In each instance, an angel saved the child's life at the last moment.
2. Jacob tricked his brother Esau into gaining his first-born status in Genesis 25. Later, his son Reuben has sex with Jacob's concubine in Genesis 35 and Jacob takes away his first-born status.
3. Jacob tricks Esau and his father Isaac by telling his father Isaac a lie to gain Isaac's blessing in Genesis 27. Later, in Genesis 29, Laban tricks him by giving him Leah instead of Rachel whom he promised to give him.
4. Jacob took advantage of his father Isaac's near blindness in Genesis 27 to gain Isaac's blessing, and his son Joseph stopped Jacob from giving his principle blessing to his older grandson in 48:10 when Jacob also had a near sightless problem.
5. Jacob showed special love for his younger son Joseph and when Jacob wanted to bless Joseph's sons in Genesis 48 and give the preferred blessing to the

younger grandson, Joseph tried to persuade his father to give it to the older one.

6. Laban kept his younger daughter from the man she loved in Genesis 29. She deprived him of his idols in Genesis 31.
7. A prince rapes Jacob's daughter Dinah. David's son who was also a prince, rapes David's daughter Tamar, his half-sister.
8. Two brothers revenged the rape of their sister Dinah and one brother, Absalom, revenged the rape of his full-sister Tamar. The brothers on both instances killed the rapist.
9. The two fathers of the raped daughters, Jacob and David, were angry that the brothers killed the rapist.
10. The Torah repeatedly shows that the oldest child does not get the blessing. Noah's sons Shem, Ham, and Japheth, with Shem listed first in Genesis 5:32, seems to be an exception. Shem was the ancestor of the Semites, a variation of his name. However, the rabbis explain that he was not the oldest son. That verse asserts that Noah had his sons when he was 500 years old. The rabbis maintain that 500 was an approximate number; the three were not born during the same year. Shem was born when Noah was 502 years old.
11. King David had improper adulterous sexual relations with Bat Sheva in II Samuel 11, and, as previously stated, his son had an illicit sexual relationship with his half-sister in II Samuel 13.
12. Similarly, another son, Absalom, had sexual relations with David's concubines in II Samuel 16.
13. There are similarities and differences in the sibling rivalries of Cain and Abel, of Jacob and Esau, and of Joseph and his bothers.
14. There are many stories of barrenness, births, difficulties in births with many similarities and many differences, and it is informative to compare and contrast them.

JEWISH AND NON-JEWISH VERSIONS OF A STORY

Chapter Twenty-Six
Differences between Some Jewish and Non-Jewish Tales

There are many instances where both Jews and non-Jews tell stories with some variations on the same plot. In many of these instances, the Jewish version attempts to use its version to teach Jews proper behavior. The only way to understand something is to see the similarities and differences with a seemingly same item. The following are examples.

RIP VAN WINKLE

Washington Irving (1783–1859) published "Rip Van Winkle" in 1820 and the tale became the first internationally famous American short story.[1] It made Irving internationally famous. Rip had an aversion to all kinds of profitable work. He found it impossible to keep his farm in order. He was a rather simple, lazy, good-natured, kind, lovable man to everyone except his wife who was exasperated by Rip's failure to do his chores. She henpecked poor Rip daily. However, his wife's behavior gained him universal popularity, for the constant complaints and threats of a termagant wife is worth all the sermons in the world for teaching the virtues of patience and long-suffering. Rip's only escape from the labors of the farm and the clamor of his wife was to stroll away into the woods and sit at the foot of a tree.

1. There are, of course, other stories of men sleeping for long periods. Wells's long tale "When the Sleeper Wakes" (1910) is about an Englishman who slept for 203 years and awoke to a new civilization. Herbert George Wells, *When the Sleeper Wakes* (CreateSpace Independent Publishing, 2011).

One day as he was sitting under his tree, a strange man (later identified as a ghost of a lonG-dead inhabitant of the area) approached him and enticed him to drink a delicious intoxicating liquor. Rip drank liberally and soon fell asleep.

When he awoke, he saw that everything had changed. A new stream was in the area. His beard had grown a foot longer. When he arrived at his town, he discovered that he had been asleep for twenty years. Many of his friends had died. His wife was also dead. (Rip was unsure whether he should be happy or sad about his newfound freedom.) His son, now grown was as lazy and unproductive as he had been. His daughter was married, and brought Rip to live at her house. Rip found a place to sit daily on the bench at the door of the local inn.

There are many versions of such tales in various cultures. The following is a Jewish version.

HONI HAMAAGEL

Honi HaMaagel (Honi the circle maker) was an especially pious Jewish man who lived during the first century BCE. The Talmud states that he was so pious that he had a special relationship with God and was able to work miracles.[2] He prayed for rain when the populace needed the precipitation. He would draw a circle, step inside it, and inform God that he would not step out of the circle until it rained. Due to his piety, he was always successful; God did not want to see this pious man stranded in a circle.

According to Talmud,[3] while traveling Honi saw a man planting a karob tree. He asked him, "How long would it take [for this tree] to bear fruit?" The man answered, "Seventy years." He then asked, "Are you sure that you will live another seventy years?" The man answered, "No. But I'm not planting this [tree] for myself, but for the next generation and the ones that follow." Honi shrugged his shoulders and left. Later, when he sat down to rest, he slept for seventy years. When he awoke and retraced his prior walk, he saw a man plucking karobs from a tree. He asked, "Did you plant this tree?" The man answered, "No. My grandfather planted it. My father told me that his father planted this tree for me."

---

2. Babylonian Talmud, *Ta'anit* 19a and 23a.
3. *Ta'anit* 23a.

SIMILARITIES

1. Both stories focus on men well-liked by their communities.
2. Both subjects sleep for an unusual length of time and awaken to see changes in their surroundings.

DIFFERENCES

1. Rip was lazy, did little to help his wife and nothing to aid his community. Honi devoted himself to helping the general population.
2. Honi was pious and loved by God because of his piety. Rip only thought of leisure.
3. Rip's story does not mention God.
4. Rip slept for twenty years, one generation, while Honi slept for seventy years, using the number seven that appears frequently in Jewish tales, which makes it possible for readers to see the impact of the action taken in the story two generations after the first act.
5. Rip's wife is disparaged in his tale. No women appear in Honi's adventure.
6. Rip does not change. He was lazy before he slept and lazy when he awoke. He did not contribute to his fellow citizens before or after the sleep. Honi changed. He did not seem to understand why the man planted a tree for a future generation before he slept; he left the man shrugging his shoulders. Later, the story tells the impact upon the man's family, and presumably, both the reader and Honi learn a lesson from what they saw/read.
7. Rip's story is fun to read but has no lesson for the reader. Honi's tale teaches a profound lesson.

Chapter Twenty-Seven
The Biblical and a Greek Creation Story

Just as the simple tales told above show that the Jews frequently wanted to place a moral lesson in their stories, the biblical tales are frequently similar to ancient myths, but Scripture tells its version of the tale to teach a moral and religious lesson. Thus, for example, Greek and Jewish myths, reports, and stories appear at first blush to be remarkably similar, but there are stark differences in how each culture views God, the world, the presence of evil, the worth of people, their duty and their future. An examination of these similarities and differences yields a keener understanding of Judaism. Just as it is beneficial to compare seemingly similar biblical tales, it is beneficial to compare biblical stories with ancient myths.

THE MYTH OF PROMETHEUS AND PANDORA IS PESSIMISTIC

The ancient Greek herdsman Hesiod (eighth century BCE) writes that muses inspired him to write poetry. He contends that evil fell upon the earth in a fit of spite by the unsympathetic god Zeus to punish humans for two good deeds performed by the Titan Prometheus for their benefit, even though they are personally innocent. Titans like Prometheus were legendary ancient deities who were beaten, banished, and later controlled by Zeus who became the chief god.

Hesiod reports that Prometheus is the wisest of the Titans; his name means "forethought." He is one of the few remaining of his breed, and as a master craftsman, he maintains that it was he and not the god Zeus that created humans out of clay as an act of goodwill, and to vex Zeus.

Prometheus, enamored by the people that he creates, likes them far more than the multitude of Greek gods. He learns many useful arts from the gods and passes them on to his creatures.

It happened once that Prometheus saw people offering a sacrifice to the gods. He calls them over and separates the sacrifice into two parts. He places the meat of the burned animal in one hide, but covers it with tripe, the most worthless parts of an animal. He puts bones in a second bag and covers it with a rich enticing layer of fat.

He calls Zeus and offers him the choice of either of the two. Zeus is deceived. He "judges a book by its cover" and selects the bag of bones, which has a cover of glistening fat.

Zeus opens the hide and is enraged. As punishment, he makes people who had lived a carefree life, and who had not had to work to produce food, earn their living through hard toil.

Prometheus does nothing to soften the punishing toil, but ever solicitous for his creatures, he steals fire from heaven and brings it to them.

Zeus, outraged by Prometheus's new actions, decides to punish him. He has a lower god make a woman called Pandora. She is beautiful and irresistible, but full of trouble. She is foolish, mischievous and idle; the first, says Hesiod, in a long line of such women. The meaning of Pandora's name, according to the myth in Hesiod's *Works and Days*, is "all-gifted." However, some scholars say that Pandora means "all-giving." Zeus sends her to Epimetheus, Prometheus's brother, but wise Prometheus warns him not to take any gifts from the gods, and he sends Pandora back.

Zeus is furious. He decides to punish Prometheus himself. He has Prometheus chained to a mountain pillar and sends a ravenous vulture to pluck at his liver every day for years. At night, when the vulture flies off, Prometheus freezes by the mountain frost, and his liver grows back ready for the next day's torture.

Epimetheus, seeing how his brother is so cruelly punished and fearful for his own safety, rushes to Zeus and begs for Pandora's hand in marriage. His request is granted. Pandora comes with a box. When Epimetheus opens the box, out springs sorrows, diseases, old age, labor, sickness, insanity, vice, and passion. Zeus has again inflicted his revenge upon humanity. Unfortunately, for Epimetheus and humanity, Zeus slams the box shut before everything escapes. Hope remains in the box. According to Hesiod, people now have no hope.

SIMILARITIES

1. Both Biblical and Greek stories seem to want to explain what people see and think about this world and their role in it.
2. The two speak about a relationship between humans and God. In both people are trying to placate God – that is, bribe the divine favor – by offering sacrifices, and God is not satisfied. No reason is narrated in Genesis why God rejected Cain's sacrifice; however, it is interesting that Abel's accepted sacrifice was an animal with its fat, while Cain offered produce.
3. The fat of a sacrificed animal is important in Greek culture and in Judaism. Zeus is deceived because he wanted the fat of the sacrifice and the biblical book of Leviticus requires that the fat burn on the altar for God. Also, as indicated above, the first acceptable sacrifice mentioned in the Torah, by Abel, has the animal's fat.
4. Prometheus, the hero of the Greek legend, bears the name that means "forethought," thereby emphasizing the importance of thinking before one acts. According to Maimonides, this is the "image of God" mentioned in Genesis, the item that distinguishes people from all other of God's creations.
5. Toil in the two tales was imposed upon people as punishment.
6. Fire is significant in both cultures. In the myth, it appears as a divine article. In the Bible, the Israelites are told not to use fire on the Sabbath. Many Bible commentators understand this mandated prohibition because the igniting of a fire is an act of creation, and Jews desist from performing acts of creation on the Sabbath to recall that God ceased creating on that day.
7. Deception is a repeating theme in both the Bible and the Greek myth. In the Bible, for example, the snake deceives Eve; Joseph's brothers lie to their father Jacob and assert that he died after they sold him into slavery; Joseph hides his identity from his brothers when they come to Egypt to buy food. In Hesiod's fable, Prometheus tricks Zeus to keep more of the sacrificial meat for people. In the Bible, people also try to trick God on occasions, but it is more respectful, subtle and indirect. Cain dissembles by asking "Am I my brother's keeper?" Adam and Eve try to hide from God in the Garden of Eden after eating the forbidden fruit.

DIFFERENCES

1. The biblical account is from God, but Hesiod's tale is the work of an inspired herdsman.
2. God, not a vengeful Titan or anything else, creates humanity in the Bible.
3. In Hesiod's fable, Prometheus creates a group of people simultaneously. The first humans in Scripture are one male and one female. The rabbis say that a larger crowd was not created to preclude individuals from maintaining that they are descended from the better first beings; instead, all people of all races and cultures descend from one pair.
4. In the Bible, man comes from the earth and the woman from his side. In Hesiod, both are born from the earth.
5. There is only one God in Judaism.
6. Unlike the Greek myth, there are no beings in the Bible that are greater than man, but lower than God (although, of course, there are Jews who believe in angels and demons).
7. The way Prometheus needs to help people presupposes that humans are resourceless. The Bible recognizes that people have the tendency to make wrong decisions (as they did in the Garden of Eden, shortly after creation). However, the Bible also insists that people can and should improve themselves.
8. The biblical God does not punish Cain for bringing an inadequate sacrifice but for murder: showing that humans are important in the Bible.
9. Maimonides, who argued that God does not want sacrifices and only allowed offerings as a concession to appease the needs of people, would probably point out, as a difference, that Zeus wants the sacrifice in the Greek tale and is furious when he does not get it.
10. Scripture as understood by Jews teaches that people are not punished for the deeds of others, unlike the myth where the people are repeatedly punished for Prometheus's acts.
11. Humans learn useful arts from the Titan Prometheus in the Greek tale but must struggle to learn it themselves in Genesis, and it takes generations to do so.
12. Both emphasize the role of the woman in bringing misfortune to humanity. However, the Greek legend stresses that the god uses her to hurt people and that the harm she brought was from a magical box. In Judaism, the woman

sent by God is not to punish Adam, but to be his helpmate. The Hebrew *eizer kenegdo*, literally "a help by his side," suggests that she is an equal. The punishment for eating the fruit of the forbidden tree pertains to both because both, not the woman alone, act improperly. The misfortunes that follow the misdeed, Genesis makes clear, are not magical; they are part of natural law: pain in childbirth and difficulties in daily work.

13. Hesiod lists all kinds of evils that descend upon people because Zeus wants to punish them. The only item that could have softened the blow was hope, but Zeus seals Pandora's box, stopping people from having this solace. There are all kinds of theories in Judaism about the origin of evil. Maimonides's approach is radically different from Hesiod's pessimism. He contends that God is good and produces only good. Evil, he insists, comes from one of three sources: (1) The laws of nature are good for the universe as a whole, but may harm individuals and groups. (2) People harm one another. (3) Individuals are frequently not careful and harm themselves.
14. The legend ends in a pessimistic tone: there is no hope. As it began with powerless people, so it ends. It seems to suggest that all that people can do is sit back and suffer. No action will help those who are feeble, incapable, and resourceless in humanity. Judaism speaks of the coming of a messianic age that people can produce by their work.

SUMMARY

By examining the Greek myth about Prometheus and comparing it to the Genesis creation story, the differences between the two stand out in stark relief. Hesiod's view of the world is pessimistic. He sees the gods selfishly seeking their own enjoyment and harming any individual that attempts to interfere. His myth depicts people as powerless beings who need external help. He envisions no hope for humanity. Judaism, in contrast, sees people possessing power – since formed in the image of God – with the duty to work to produce a perfect world.

Hesiod's myth, in short, gives a fantastic fatalistic explanation of the presence of evil in the word and offers no remedy. The Bible, in contrast, lists practices that can improve individuals and produce a better world.

Chapter Twenty-Eight
The Biblical and Roman Creation Story

As previously stated, it is basic psychology that people cannot understand a subject unless they understand its similarity and opposite. In fact, this was the first lesson I learnt at Johns Hopkins University in my first psychology class.

Peter Kamara's *Ancient Roman Mythology* contains a description of a Roman creation myth. It is interesting to read the striking similarities between the Roman version of creation and what the Bible states. This will open our eyes to much that we did not see in the biblical creation story.

SIMILARITIES

1. Both say that before the establishment of the world there was chaos, but while the Bible does not describe the chaos, the myth states that the elements of air, earth, fire, and sea mixed as one. The confusion resolved itself by fire as the lightest, rising up and becoming the heavens. Air became the level below heaven. Earth was set below the air, and water, being the heaviest element, was set below everything.
2. The sequence of events in Scripture and the myth are remarkably similar. Initially, humans lived in a golden age. Nature provided all that was necessary. This is similar to the story of the Garden of Eden. The golden age followed the silver age when there were extremes in temperature and man needed to wear clothes and cultivate the ground. In the Bible, Adam and Eve put on clothes after eating the forbidden fruit and Adam thereafter needed to cultivate the ground. The Bronze Age followed with the beginning of crime

and the division of the people. This reflects the sequence in the Bible: Cain killing Abel and the building of the Tower of Babel. The Iron Age followed in which greed proliferated and there was war. Abraham was involved in such a war in Genesis 14.

3. The gods were displeased with human activities and decided to destroy them. As with Noah's flood, the gods flooded the earth by sea and storm. Only Mount Parnassus was not flooded. Only two Titans, Deucalion and his wife Pyrrha who led a blameless life were spared.

DIFFERENCES

1. There were many gods. They had human attributes, including a strong sexual drive. They often bedded and fought one another.
2. Titans, the offspring of Gaia (earth) and Uranus (heaven), were created before the humans and had enormous strengths. One of the Titans, Prometheus, took some earth and created males, not women, and formed the men in the shape of the gods. The Bible does not say there was a race of human-like beings (Titans) who existed before humans and for part of the human existence. The Bible states that God created humans, not Titans. Yet both say humans were created from earth with something about God in their being. In the Bible humans also had "the image of God," which has been variously interpreted. Maimonides states it is that God gave them intelligence.[1]
3. While the Greek myth has Prometheus giving humans fire, the Roman myth attributes the gift to the goddess Minerva who stole the fire from heaven and brought it to the men. They were then able to make tools and weapons and introduce trade. The Bible has no tale about the introduction of fire. However, it also indicates that the making of weapons and tools did not occur until the seventh generation of humans after Adam and Eve, invented by a descendant of Cain.[2]
4. Jupiter, the supreme god, disliked that humans had fire. So, he sent Pandora to earth. She had found in the possession of Epimetheus, Prometheus's brother a box containing war, plague, pestilence, and the like. As long as the

1. Maimonides, Guide of the Perplexed, 1:1.
2. Genesis 4:22.

box remained closed, there was no problem. However, like many women, Pandora was curious. She opened the box thus releasing these problems upon the earth. Thus, as in the Bible, it is a woman who brings difficulties to man. Unlike the Bible, Pandora's box is designed to explain how evil was created. It states that the god caused it by sending Pandora. The Bible gives no reason for evil in the world. It states in Genesis 1 that everything created was good. The narratives in the Bible show humans creating evils and their consequences.

5. There was a flood as in the Bible. All humans died. Only two Titans survived. After the flood, the two surviving Titans went to a temple and an oracle told them how to create new humans. They were to cast stones on the earth from which humanity arose. Scripture does not say that only two Titans survived who recreated humans by throwing stones; Noah and his family were saved and all humanity is descendant from them.

SUMMARY

What should we conclude from the many similarities between the myths and Scripture? The myth is without doubt, a fable. A myth is a fictional traditional story, especially one concerning the early history of a people, or explaining some natural or social phenomenon, and typically involving supernatural beings or events. While untrue, it is what Plato called a "noble lie," and what Maimonides termed "an essential truth," necessary to make the masses feel good. It helps the general population understand life, how it began, its purpose, why there is evil in the world, will life turn out well for me, and the like. Should we understand that the biblical creation story is also a myth? Whether or not it is a myth, why is it included in the Bible?

The Gilgamesh myth adds an additional question. Since composed before the Bible, did the Bible draw on it to compose its version of the flood?

Chapter Twenty-Nine
The Biblical Flood and the Gilgamesh Myth

There are remarkable similarities between the biblical story of the flood and the more ancient version of Gilgamesh. The Babylonian epic Gilgamesh, written on twelve tablets around 2000 BCE before the time of Moses, has survived several versions. It was discovered in 1839 among the ruins of a buried library in the excavated ancient city Nineveh. Amazingly, the author's name, Shin-eqi-unninni is written in one of the tablets. He is the oldest known author. It is worth exploring what Gilgamesh tells us about the flood because it helps us understand the biblical view of God and man better.

UTNAPISHTIM'S ACCOUNT OF THE FLOOD

In the eleventh of the twelve tablets, Utnapishtim tells Gilgamesh about the flood. The gods created humans, Utnapishtim explains, but they soon recognized that they had made a mistake. Humans became so numerous that the gods were unable to stand the noise. They met in counsel and decide to rid the world of the clattering humans by washing them away with a flood. The chief god insisted that the other gods swear that they would not reveal the destruction to humans. Ea, one of the gods who was previously involved in creating the humans, warned King Utnapishtim by not talking to him directly, as required by his oath, but by talking to Utnapishtim's wall while Utnapishtim was in the room. Ea advised him to build a large, square boat and bring all living things into it. Utnapishtim loaded the boat with gold and silver, his wife, and a sampling of all living things.

The flood lasted seven days and seven nights until the boat settled on a mountaintop, where it remained for seven days. Utnapishtim released a dove to discover whether the water had waned, but the dove returned, showing that the land was still flooded. Later, he sent a swallow with the same result. Finally, he dispatched a raven, and the raven did not return, for the water had receded.

As soon as Utnapishtim exited the boat, he offered a sheep as a sacrifice to the gods and a libation (meat and wine). The gods liked the sacrifices so much that they regreted having murdered the humans. They gave Utnapishtim and his wife a gift of immortal life as an act of contrition.

UTNAPISHTIM'S ADVICE TO GILGAMESH ABOUT IMMORTAL LIFE

Utnapishtim tells his descendant that he will achieve eternal life if he can stay awake for seven nights. Gilgamesh tries but falls asleep the first night. Utnapishtim's wife feels sorry for him and persuades her husband to tell him about a plant that, while not giving eternal life, could make him young again. Gilgamesh finds the plant but, when he leaves it unguarded, a serpent eats it. Therefore, snakes shed their skin and become young again.

SIMILARITIES

1. Gilgamesh is described as partly divine and Scripture portrays humans as being born in the "image of God."
2. Both stories portray humans as knowledgeable beings, and in both stories, humans do not always use the intelligence they were given.
3. The number seven occurs frequently in the Gilgamesh story and in the Bible (the Sabbath is the seventh day; Passover and Sukkot last seven days, etc.).
4. The number twelve occurs often in both the myth and the Bible, where many biblical figures have twelve sons.
5. A splendid garden appears in both stories. The gardens contain the potential to grant eternal life.
6. In both tales, the protagonists are unable to obtain eternal life.
7. Both heroes survive the flood in a boat/ark.
8. Both the ark and the boat finally rest on a mountaintop.
9. Noah and Utnapishtim send out birds on more than one occasion to discover whether the land is still flooded.

10. Both men offer a sacrifice when they descend from their ark/boat, although Noah "took from every clean cattle and every clean fowl and offered burnt offerings on the altar [that he built]," while Utnapishtim offered a sheep and a wine libation.

DIFFERENCES

1. As in most pagan myths, the gods behave in improper ways and leave humans no real freedom to act: the humans are subject to the will and whims of the gods. In the Bible, people have the power to make decisions and are encouraged to use that power properly.
2. Gilgamesh is the leader of his people and a warrior. Noah was neither.
3. While Gilgamesh is so barbaric that the gods need to control him, the Bible states that Noah was perfect in his generation.
4. The Babylonian myth emphasizes the pursuit of pleasure, while the Genesis story emphasizes the importance of proper conduct.
5. Gilgamesh is fearful of dying, but Noah expressed no fear.
6. The principle theme of the Gilgamesh epic is the hero's attempt to find eternal life. Eternal life is not the central part of the story in the Bible.
7. Both the Bible and the Babylonian tale describe a plant/tree that gives life and a serpent that interferes with the future of humanity. However, the biblical account of the tree has nothing to do with the flood, but with the initial creation story in the Garden of Eden.
8. The trees in the Gilgamesh garden bear precious gems, while the biblical trees bear food.
9. The principle theme of Gilgamesh and the garden is eternal life. While the Garden of Eden contains a tree of life, it plays a minor role in the story.
10. God stops Adam and Eve from eating from the tree of life, and expels them from the garden before they can eat from it. Gilgamesh has the opportunity to receive eternal life, but is unable to perform the task required to achieve it.
11. In the Bible, God decides to destroy people because they are acting improperly. God saves Noah and his family because they act justly. In the myth, the gods decide to wipe out humanity because of the noise they produce. The first story focuses on proper behavior; the second on the gods' selfish pleasure. The myth's divine intention is to wipe out all humanity.

12. Noah does not try to save gold and silver on his ark.
13. Noah's ark is not square.
14. Noah takes his entire family with him, while Utnapishtim only brings his wife.
15. The flood in Gilgamesh lasts seven days and seven nights. Noah's flood begins seven days after Noah enters the ark but lasts for forty days and forty nights.
16. Noah sends a raven first, then a dove twice. The dove later became a symbol of peace. Utnapishtim releases a dove, which finds no place to land, then a swallow with the same result, and finally a raven, which doesn't return, revealing that it had a place to land and food to eat. The raven is a symbol of violence.
17. Noah does not offer wine as a sacrifice, but drinks it himself.

SUMMARY

There are remarkable similarities between the Gilgamesh myth and the Bible. The details in both accounts are very close. This leads one to think that the idea of the flood and its details were well-known in ancient times and the Bible used the ancient accounts to teach its own lessons.

The story of the flood is in only one of Gilgamesh's twelve tablets. The other tablets contain details that are like other parts of the Bible.

Yet, there are many differences; the result is the varied worldview that the Bible expresses. The two texts have very different ideas about how God/gods function; how the divine feel about people; how the divine treat humanity; and how people should behave toward each other and toward the divine. The similarities and differences should help us see the significance of the Noah story better.

MAIMONIDES

Chapter Thirty
Skepticism Can Be Good

Although I am an observant Orthodox Jew, I agree with Aristotle and Maimonides that the basic obligation of humans is to use their intelligence, not sit passively and pray.[1] Human intelligence is the *tzelem Elohim*, the image of God that God placed in humans when they were created. I also agree with Rabbi Abraham Yitzhak Kook (1865–1935),[2] that we can and should learn much from atheists because they have some good ideas and they make us think. The purpose of the Torah, as Maimonides taught, is to prompt us to learn some basic truths and to use our intelligence to improve society and ourselves.[3]

THE PROBLEMS WITH FAITH

Two PhD scientists, teaching in two Israeli universities, Maor Kohn and Mati Cohen, both atheists, have just published *A Beginner's Guide to Skepticism.*[4] They discuss the weaknesses of faith because it is detached from the accumulated knowledge and evidence-based objective reality, and accepts as true what science,

1. Maimonides, *Guide of the Perplexed*, 1:1.
2. Discussed in: Pinchas Polonsky, *Religious Zionism of Rav Kook* (CreateSpace, 2017). Rabbi Kook taught that Orthodox Jews must preserve the practices of their religion – this is Orthodoxy. However, Orthodox Jews must also incorporate the new information that the world reveals – this is Modernism. The two together yield Modern Orthodoxy.
3. Maimonides, *Guide of the Perplexed* 3:28, 3:54, and other sites.
4. Maor Kohn and Mati Cohen, *A Beginner's Guide to Skepticism* (Simple Story, 2019).

the senses, and logic dismiss as wrong, and it bases life upon subjective emotional reality.

They remind us that Karl Marx noted, "Religion is the opium of the people."[5] "The church and state can use religion to manage large groups of people and make them act contrary to their natural, animalistic behavior... such as sending thousands of people to die in the crusades for the church."[6]

Miracles, the authors point out, are not the intervention of God in human life, but "a statistically rare event and not a supernatural matter."[7] Prayer is not a conversation with God, but "a prayer is to help educate a person... through intellectual and rational self-examination."[8] "Prayers work only when science works."[9] Prayer cannot grow a limb.

Faith fills emotional psychological batteries. It creates a "peace of mind, equanimity, meaning, a purpose or life, a sense of comfort and consolation."[10] It removes our fear of death, for we will live after we die and receive a reward. It connects us to something magnificent. It increases our self-esteem. It gives us answers to negative events. We do not have to think. As Rabbi Soloveitchik who extolled faith taught in all of his writings, all we need to do is surrender ourselves to God. Religion acts as an opium for most people in allowing them to violate what Maimonides taught that the Torah demands: they sit back, pray, and do not use their intelligence to improve themselves and society. Faith is the opposite of knowledge. Many go to clergy to solve life's problems but have sufficient sense not to let a plumber conduct open-heart surgery.

Is there a similarity between faith and the young man or woman who sits before a famous painting spending every day contemplating it, enjoying its beauty, reading and rereading the essay beneath the art work, but never being all that he or she can be?

---

5. Karl Marx, "A contribution to the Critique of Hegel's Philosophy of Right," (*Deutsch-Französische Jahrbücher*, 1844).
6. Kohn and Cohen, *A Beginner's Guide to Skepticism*, 27.
7. Ibid., 62.
8. *Guide of the Perplexed* 3:51, quoted by Kohn and Cohen on Ibid., 62.
9. Ibid., 64.
10. Ibid., 33.

THE VALUE OF SCIENCE

While faith is what we want to see and believe, science is what intelligent people have found through experiments and logic to be true.

The authors tell us why we should accept science even though it is based on statistics, is only a theory, and the conclusions often change. They also talk about subjects such as what is God; Bible stories; morality in the Bible; miracles; reward and punishment; tradition; the difference between faith and belief; what makes one religion better than another, and similar subjects.

They also show that people who claim that faith and science do not contradict one another are wrong, and explain that people who think that faith and science can coexist reconcile the contradiction because of a psychological phenomenon called cognitive dissonance. "I know that what I am doing is not worthy/moral/right/reasonable/logical. But I convince myself in a very creative way of the need for doing it." For example, you know that smoking is harmful and will most likely kill you, but you justify your habit by relying on an isolated fact, your grandmother smoked until age ninety and died in her sleep, cancer free.

One of the problems noted by the authors is that scientists showed that "beyond reasonable doubt the theory that human beings, even under sterile and non-threatening conditions, tend to accept the authority of another person, and sometimes act in extreme ways even endangering human life." People tend to act unreasonably because they heard the idea from a man with a long beard and black hat.[11] (I saw such a rabbi deliver a sermon on two occasions in which he advised his congregants that if they fell over a cliff and were holding on to a tree with a large drop below them that would kill them, they should let go and rely on God to save them. I heard congregants say, "That makes sense to me.")

UNANSWERED QUESTIONS

The authors discuss a number of issues, which they feel do not have a satisfactory answer, and conclude that since they do not know the answer, religion must be wrong. These include: who created God? Why do we not see any indication that God exists? Why does evil exist in the world? Why do people and animals suffer? Why did God kill animals in the Flood? Why did God destroy first-borns as a

11. Ibid., 80.

tenth plague in Egypt? Why are many children born with medical problems such as autism? How can we accept the Bible as the truth when it includes a tale of a talking snake with legs? How do we deal with seeming inconsistencies in Scripture? Are there not questionable immoral commands in the Torah? Do LGBTQ people not have rights? Are women disparaged in Judaism?[12]

WHAT SHOULD ONE DO?

Drs. Kohn and Cohen offer what they consider an alternative to religion. They teach, "One should not treat others in ways that they would not like to be treated."[13] We should try to understand what another person wants and does not want and act accordingly. Learn to cooperate with others. It brings prosperity, wealth, education, and peace. Respect every person, regardless of religion, gender, sexual orientation, age, and culture. Be good to all. Respect animals; they also have feelings. Do not depend on beliefs. "The more people believe, the more they harm the act of creation."[14] Recognize that heaven is here on earth, for not caring for it results in our banishment. Do not be fooled by clergy. "Acquire as much education and knowledge as possible. It is a privilege and not a burden to learn new things."[15]

Arguably, these alternative teachings are the teachings that Judaism has taught for centuries. Instead of disagreeing with them, it is best to have reminders and encouragement to do them.

Aristotle and Maimonides emphasize that we should acquire as much education and knowledge as we can, and never stop learning. These traits are what distinguishes us from animals and plants. Failure to do so make us no better than a potted plant. Rabbi Kook also imparted that we should learn from everyone. The truth, Maimonides taught, is the truth, no matter what its source.[16]

12. See Maimonides, *Guide of the Perplexed,* where these questions are addressed.
13. Ibid., 193.
14. Ibid., 198.
15. Ibid., 206.
16. Maimonides, *Guide of the Perplexed,* Introduction.

Chapter Thirty-One
A Joke about the Origin of Faith

People who live their lives relying on faith are making a huge mistake. This not what the Torah teaches. Frequently the truth shows more clearly in a joke than in a plain statement.

THE ORIGIN OF THE NOTION THAT PEOPLE MUST HAVE FAITH

As will be discussed later, Paul introduced the notion that God wants people to have faith. During his lifetime, many of the people who later called themselves Christians were Jews, and then, they began to develop beliefs about Jesus. Paul was very interested in converting the pagans to Judaism, but faced the problem that the pagan males did not want circumcision, and neither the men nor woman wanted to accept the Jewish dietary laws. Paul told them that they need not do what other Jews do, just have faith. This joke reflects the pagan view about circumcision.

SQUIRREL PROBLEMS IN CHURCHES

The Presbyterian Church called a meeting to decide what to do about their squirrel infestation. After much prayer and consideration, they concluded that the squirrels were predestined to be there, and they should not interfere with God's divine will.

At the Baptist Church, the squirrels had taken an interest in the baptistery. The deacons met and decided to put a waterslide on the baptistery for the squirrels to drown themselves. The squirrels liked the slide and unfortunately, knew instinctively how to swim, so twice as many squirrels showed up the following week.

The Lutheran Church decided that they were not able to harm any of God's creatures. Therefore, they humanely trapped their squirrels and set them free near the Baptist church. Two weeks later the squirrels were back when the Baptists took down the waterslide.

Then the Catholic Church came up with a very creative strategy! They baptized all the squirrels and made them members of the church. Now they only see them at Christmas and Easter.

There was very little to hear from the Jewish synagogue. They took the first squirrel and circumcised him. They have not seen a squirrel since then.

Chapter Thirty-Two
Maimonides's Teaching about Eating

I wrote about Maimonides's medical teachings in my book, *Maimonides: Reason above All* and gave many examples there. Maimonides was a great philosopher and writer on Jewish laws, he practiced as a doctor, and he wrote extensively about healthy living. He taught that people who think they should eat until they feel "full" are making a huge mistake.

MAIMONIDES'S MEDICAL BOOKS

Maimonides wrote his *Commentary on the Aphorisms of Hippocrates,* one of his ten books on medicine, around the year 1195, close to ten years before his death in 1204. In the book, he offers his opinion as to which of Hippocrates's aphorisms are correct and which are wrong.

The Greek Hippocrates (c. 460–c. 377 BCE) is the most famous of all physicians and considered the father of medicine. Many people of his age, as well as for a long time after his death, considered medicine a part of religion, an involvement of the gods in the affairs of men. Hippocrates rejected this notion. Using observation and the best science of his time, he taught that diseases are not a divine punishment, nor are they the result of any other superstitious agent, such as demons, evil eyes, or animals such as black cats.

He gave the world the famous Hippocratic Oath, in which he emphasized the importance of medical ethics and careful physician treatment. The most famous part of the oath states that the doctor should do all that is reasonable to avoid harming the patient or treating the patient unjustly.

The most significant physician after Hippocrates was Galen (130–200 CE), who explained and developed Hippocrates's teachings and whose authority prevailed for fourteen hundred years. Maimonides agreed with many of Hippocrates's teachings as explained by Galen, but not all of them, as I detail in *Maimonides: Reason above All.*

MAIMONIDES'S TEACHINGS

In my book I explain how Maimonides advises how to prolong life and make life as painless and enjoyable as possible. This includes him stressing that everyone must exercise, even the elderly. The one piece of advice that I want to emphasize here is what Maimonides wrote in *Mishneh Torah, Deot,* chapter 4, halakha 2, do not eat until the stomach is full but eat only three quarters of full satisfaction.[1]

Very simply, Maimonides's advice is that eating until one feels "full" is suicide. Overeating kills about half of the people in the US today.

Scientists today have proven that Maimonides was correct. They tell us that it takes about fifteen or twenty minutes for the body to register satisfaction. We need to stop eating while we still feel hungry, and wait fifteen to twenty minutes after which we will feel satisfied.

Leaving the table feeling "full," will result in fifteen to twenty minutes that the body is overstuffed. If not controlled, this urge to feel full may actually kill us.

This teaching is very relevant: it is a matter of life and death.

ANOTHER EATING PROBLEM

While we are on the subject of overeating, a problem from which over half of the people in the US suffer, I will discuss a second eating mistake. King Henry VIII (1491–1547) is a good example. His legacy is mostly due to his six marriages, a serious problem that affected England in his day and through to today because he changed the religion in England when the Pope refused to grant him a divorce or annulment from his then wife.

Henry VIII succeeded his father Henry VII as king when he was eighteen years old. As a young man, he was very popular. Taller than the average Englishman, he was handsome, very healthy, and loved many vigorous activities including

1. See also Moses Maimonides (Rambam), *Mishneh Torah, Deot* 1:4 and 5:2 where Maimonides states one should eat no more than one's basic needs.

hunting, dancing, combat, and jousting (a sport in which two horsemen ride toward each other at full gallop, each trying to knock the other off of his horse by the force of a spear).

In 1536, Henry fell from his horse and his horse fell on top of him. He was unconscious for two hours. He injured his leg, which never healed properly, and suffered from pain in his leg for the rest of his life. Afterwards, he lived a sedentary life, giving up virtually all of his vigorous activities.

The mistake he made is applicable today. It is important to keep active when consuming a lot of food. This becomes increasing difficult as a person grows older and is less active. People need to reduce what they eat as they advance in age because of the change in their bodies, and because they are not physically active.

Henry was very active before his accident and this helped control his weight in his youth. After the accident, he still consumed the same quantity of food, thus gaining considerable weight. He was soon over 400 pounds, which convinced many scholars that his weight greatly contributed to his death when he was only fifty-five years of age.

Chapter Thirty-Three
The Bible's Fundamental Teaching Is Not What Many Think

What idea did Maimonides consider so fundamental to Judaism that he introduced his code of Jewish law, his *Mishneh Torah,* and his list of commandments with this principle? It will surprise many people to realize that it is not "faith in God." Let us initially look at the two books before we examine what Maimonides listed first in each of them.

MAIMONIDES'S *MISHNEH TORAH*

Maimonides's fourteen-volume *Mishneh Torah* was the first, most comprehensive, most readable, and best-organized code of Jewish law. The fourteen books of his code, expertly crafted have exactly one thousand chapters. The work is a rational compilation. Among much else, Marc B. Shapiro, in his *Studies in Maimonides and His Interpreters,* lists over fifty different talmudic halakhot that Maimonides omitted from his code of law because they were prompted by superstitious notions.[1]

Yet about a century after his death, another Spaniard, Jacob ben Asher (1270–c. 1340, called *Ba'al Haturim*) composed a multi-volume work on Jewish law that he called the *Tur.* Roughly two centuries later, still another Spanish rabbi, Joseph Karo (1488–1575) compiled his multi-volume law book, which he named the *Shulchan*

1. Marc B. Shapiro, *Studies in Maimonides and His Interpreters* (PA, Scranton: University of Scranton Press, 2008).

Arukh. More than half a dozen other collections followed, but the *Shulchan Arukh*, with annotations by the Polish Rabbi Moshe Isserles (1525–1572, called Ramah) became the favored code and is used by most Jews.

Why the composition of these codes after the magnificent one by Maimonides? Simply because most Jews, including Joseph Karo who believed he had frequent conversations with an angel and who wrote about what the angel told him in a book other than his code, could not accept a rational life and needed one filled with superstition. The codes of law by ben Asher, Karo, and Isserles are filled with practices based on superstition because of their inability to deal with Maimonides's rationalism, and his refusal to include superstitious practices, magical conduct, and the use of omens, mysticism and other irrational behaviors that were so dear to the general population. These non-rational behaviors were rampant among many Jews – including numerous rabbis.

Some of these behaviors included marrying only on certain days considered safe, washing hands every morning three times to remove demons that attached themselves to the hands during the night, and not spilling any of the water on the ground lest the demons remain in your house. Do not sleep facing east. Be extremely careful of the evil eye. Use salt to protect yourself from demons.

The first of the fourteen books of *Mishneh Torah* is *Sefer Hamada*, The Book of Knowledge. It begins with *yesodei haTorah*, laws which are fundamental to the Torah. What is the first fundamental law that Maimonides lists?

Maimonides starts *Mishneh Torah* with the first fundamental principal of Judaism: "The foundation of all foundations and the pillar of wisdom is to know that there is a primary being [God] who brought into being all existence." He does not say that it is basic to Judaism to believe in God, but to know that God exists. He sees this idea, indeed this command in Exodus 20:2, the Decalogue, where God tells the Israelites "I am *Y-H-V-H* your God."

MAIMONIDES'S *SEFER HAMITZVOT* (BOOK OF THE COMMANDMENTS)

The first report that the Torah contains 613 commandments dates to the third century CE, when Rabbi Simlai mentioned this concept in a sermon recorded in the Babylonian Talmud, *Makkot* 23b. The Talmud states: "Rabbi Simlai gave as a sermon (*darash Rabi Simlai*): 613 commandments were communicated to Moses – 365 negative commands, corresponding to the number of solar days (in a year), and 248 positive commands, corresponding to the number of the members [bones covered with flesh] of a man's body." Rabbi Simlai invented the number 613 because it fit his sermon: A person should observe the Torah with all his body parts (248) every day (365). The two numbers total 613. 150 years before Rabbi Simlai ben Azzai said that there were three hundred biblical commands.[2] E.E. Urbach wrote, "In the Tannaitic sources this number [613] is unknown."[3]

Maimonides not only knew that the notion of 613 biblical commands is only sermonic, but that the general population accepted the notion, and that they wanted information about what Judaism required, and what it prohibited, so he listed the commandments that he felt the rabbis considered either explicit or implicit in the Torah.

Maimonides states in his *Sefer Hamitzvot* that the first command is *haamin* (generally translated "believe") that there is a supreme cause that is the creator of everything in existence. However, in his list of commandments in his *Mishneh Torah,* Maimonides uses the words "know" when he lists the commandments, not "believe."

In Nachmanides's *Hasagot,* he comments on Maimonides's commandments, and refers readers to *Mekhilta Chodesh* 6. He tells readers that *haamin,* usually translated "believe," means accepting God and nothing else as a divinity; it is like a king who tells his subjects first *know* that I am your ruler then you will know that I can give you commands that you must obey. Similarly, Rabbi David Altschuler (called Radbaz, c. 1479–c. 1573) states in his *Metzudat David* that what is meant is the command to know God.

Virtually all scholars agree that Maimonides opines that people need to learn to know God. For example, Steve Harvey speaks about the human goal being

---

2. *Sifrei* Deuteronomy, 76.

3. Ephraim E. Urbach, *The Sages: Their Concepts and Beliefs,* trans. Israel Abrahams (Cambridge, MA: Harvard University Press, 1987). See also Israel Drazin, *Mysteries of Judaism II: Common sense Evaluations of Religious Thoughts* (Jerusalem: Gefen Publishing House, 2017), chapter 23, "There are not 613 biblical commands," for more information on this subject, including the views of sages agreeing the 613 is sermonic, not real.

"apprehension of God."[4] Isadore Twersky states "'Knowing God' is both a refrain and a leitmotif of all Maimonidean writing; it is a goal and a means."[5]

WHY IS BELIEF IN GOD NOT THE GOAL?

It is not rational to expect people to believe in God. First, no one can force another to believe in anything. Second, believing and faith are not reasonable. Faith is accepting as true what science, one's senses, and logic tells us is untrue. To take what Søren Aabye Kierkegaard called a "leap of Faith" over a deep dangerous cavern makes as much sense as jumping into one's death in the depth of the cavern. Third, there is no requirement to believe in the Torah. The word *emunah*, which came to mean "faith" in Modern Hebrew, is in the Bible, but in the Bible, it means holding steadfast, keeping one's worship of God not idols. It refers to behavior not thought. Fourth, accepting the notion of belief and faith is accepting a Christian concept. As noted in chapter 31, in the first century CE, Paul wanted to convert pagans to Judaism, for Christianity at that time was a group among Jews. When the pagans refused because they did not want to be circumcised, or restricted in certain acts such as what they could eat, Paul told them that they could refrain from the Jewish behaviors if they believed in Jesus.

THE TORAH EXPLAINS HOW TO GAIN KNOWLEDGE OF GOD

Moses asked God to tell him how he could know God in Exodus 33:18–23. Moses requests God: "Show me please Your glory," meaning, "show me what You are." God replies that He will make the divine goodness pass before Moses…, but tells him that he cannot see God's face. Moses should stand behind a rock…, but after God passes "you will see my back, but my face will not be seen."

Some commentators explain this with another metaphor. It is as if Moses can only see God's footprints after God passes by.

God is telling Moses that because human intelligence is limited, humans are incapable of understanding what God is. However, they can understand much about God by seeing and understanding what God has done, seeing God's "back."

---

4. In Joel L. Kraemer, *Perspectives on Maimonides* (The Littman Library of Jewish civilization, 1996), 66–67.

5. Isadore Twersky, *Introduction to the Code of Maimonides* (New Haven, CT: Yale University Press, 1980), 261.

What is it that humans can see? Humans can see what God created by what exists on earth and in the laws of nature.

Once we understand that the only way to know God is to know how the world functions, we understand that the fundamental teaching of the Torah, what God wants us to do, is to study the sciences.[6]

6. Many scholars have recognized this. See for example, Herbert A. Davidson, *Maimonides the Rationalist* (The Littman Library of Jewish Civilization, 2011). His first chapter is entitled "The Study of Philosophy as a Religious Obligation" where he speaks about "grounding love of God in scientific knowledge."

Chapter Thirty-Four
How Later Rabbis Distorted Maimonides's Teachings

The "Yeshiva world," is comprised for the most part of schools where far-right rabbis teach Jewish students their view of Judaism, a religion that rejects secular studies as harmful and heretical. Many far-right rabbis respect Maimonides's *Mishneh Torah*, his code of Jewish laws, but not his philosophical *Guide of the Perplexed*, since he bases his *Guide* on secular studies and encourages people of all religions to learn about the world. Some go so far to claim that Maimonides did not write the *Guide*, and most tell their students not to read it. When they encounter a Maimonidean idea and write or speak about it, what they say does not reflect the brilliant teachings of "the great eagle," but as Professor Menachem Kellner wisely states, what they see in Maimonides is a mirror where they see their own ideas, not those of the great sage.

REINVENTING MAIMONIDES

Professors James A. Diamond and Menachem Kellner are two highly respected experts on Maimonides. They wrote three and four articles, respectively, in the 2019 book *Reinventing Maimonides in Contemporary Jewish Thought*.[1] In this book,

1. James Arthur Diamond, Menachem Kellner, and Seth Kadish, *Reinventing Maimonides in Contemporary Jewish Thought* (Liverpool: The Littman Library of Jewish Civilization, Liverpool, 2019).

they describe the views of eight rabbis, Naftali Tzvi Yehudah Berlin (1816–1893), Joseph B. Soloveitchik (1903–1993), Abraham Yitzhak Kook (1865–1935), Kalonymus Kalman Shapira (1889–1943), Elhanan Wasserman (1874–1941), Aharon Kotler (1891–1962), Shlomo Aviner (born 1943), and Joseph Kafih (1917–2000). The following are some examples of how they all, except for Kafih, misrepresented Maimonides.

RABBI NAFTALI TZVI YEHUDAH BERLIN

James A. Diamond tells readers that Maimonides respected all people and even used ideas he learnt from the pagan philosopher Aristotle. Rabbi Berlin was only tolerant of non-Jews and secular Jews because he felt they were involved in errant behavior, and he was tolerant only because of his "deep seated aversion to communal strife."[2] Maimonides's views sacrifices as a pagan ritual from which monotheists be incrementally weaned, while for Berlin, it is a sign of spiritual virtue that is beneficial if it is regulated. He also disagreed with Maimonides view that all the biblical commands are rational and insisted that the opposite is true; they are all irrational. He rejected Maimonides's teaching that all people, including Jews have a primary duty to develop their intelligence and know God, and care for the needs of the community. Maimonides saw the goal of the biblical commands as practical: inculcating correct opinions, moral qualities and political civic actions, but Berlin focused only on the spiritual. Yet, despite the differences, Rabbi Berlin felt that Maimonides agreed with him.

RABBI JOSEPH B. SOLOVEITCHIK

Menachem Kellner tells us that Rabbi Soloveitchik also disagreed with Maimonides and devalued knowledge as aiding people. He insisted that religious behaviors not knowledge lead to love of God. Chasidism influenced him as did the idea that all commands are irrational, and he argued that people must have faith that God knows what is good and obey the commands. Holiness to Mai-

2. As an Army Brigadier General, I lectured to military chaplains that it is not enough to tolerate people of other religions. "Would you turn over in your bed at home toward your wife and say, 'Dear, I tolerate you.'"

monides depends on how people act on earth, but it was something unearthly to Soloveitchik. He insisted that when Maimonides spoke about knowing God, he meant believing in God. He rejected the recognition by his friend Rabbi Chaim Heller (1879–1960) and his son-in-law Rabbi Isadore Twersky (1930–1997) that Maimonides meant what he said. He insisted that people must "surrender," "give oneself up to God," "merge with God." Most significantly, the consensus is that Maimonides was emphasizing that it is important that all people of all religions develop their intelligence and knowledge by studying the sciences, learn to be all that the person can be and help improve society. However, Rabbi Soloveitchik mischaracterized Maimonides, and stated that Maimonides focused on Jews and encouraged Jews to surrender themselves and observe the halakha, Jewish law.

RABBI ABRAHAM ISAAC KOOK

James A. Diamond wrote that Rabbi Abraham Isaac Kook, like Rabbi Soloveitchik was mystical. He translated Maimonides's philosophy into a new philosophical mysticism. Like the others and contrary to Maimonides, he argued that rational thought cannot adequately accommodate the "fullness of the holy" required by the Torah. He had enormous respect for Maimonides and considered his reworking and derationalizing of Maimonides as a true natural extension of Maimonides's thought.

SUMMARY

In short, these rabbis could not conceive that a brilliant rabbinic figure like Maimonides could have had any idea that was contrary to the far-right notions they championed. Therefore, they did not openly oppose Maimonides, but they forcefully promoted anti-Maimonidean notions and attributed them to Maimonides. It is important when reading the views of such rabbis to realize that they are not telling us what Maimonides actually said.

OTHER IDEAS

Chapter Thirty-Five
Greeks, like Jews, Did Not Have the Concept of "Sin"

I have often mentioned two things: (1) the brilliance of Maimonides and (2) that in the Hebrew Bible there is no concept of "sin" as it is understood today, as a distorting stain upon the soul that requires a kind of supernatural atonement process. Furthermore, the concept of "sin" is Christian and I feel that it is harmful. Jews mistakenly came to believe that Judaism accepts a thing called "sin," without realizing it was not Jewish, because "sin" is mentioned so frequently, and they think it applied to Adam, Eve, and others in the Hebrew Bible. Now I wish to impart a third idea.

THE JEWISH VIEW OF SIN

Improper behavior in Judaism is a natural event. The Hebrew Bible speaks of three categories of misdeeds that are not synonyms. There is *chet,* the misstep, literally "missing the mark," as if one were shooting an arrow at a target, and hitting instead the outer rims thus missing its center. The Bible mentions it 34 times. The second, *pesha,* occurring 93 times, is a conscious rebellious act such as taking revenge, stealing, and murder. The third *avon,* cited in 233 instances, is an error, an unintentional act that nevertheless has harmful consequences. Understood in this natural way, it should be clear that the conduct is something that should not provoke long-standing feelings of guilt and prayerful recitations; individuals should recognize what they did wrong, think why they did the wrong, and take actions that remedy the consequences to assure that there will be no repetition.

The second idea that I stressed for decades is the brilliance of Maimonides, Judaism's smartest thinker since the lawgiver Moses. I liked that he taught that the truth is the truth no matter what its source. He told us in his introduction to his *Guide of the Perplexed* that he relied on the wisdom of the ancient pagan philosopher Aristotle for many of his ideas. Maimonides explained *chet* and how to deal with it as stated above. *Chet* is a behavior to correct, and not agonize over.

A NEW IDEA

Every day I look forward to getting my free "Word of the Day" sent directly to my email inbox. (The website is "Dictionary.com.") I was surprised that on April 3, 2019, the word for the day taught a lesson about "sin." The word was hamartia.; flaw.

In the "Origin" of the word section, Word of the Day wrote: "In Greek the noun hamartíā means 'failure, fault, error (of judgment), guilt, sin.' Hamartia, if familiar at all, will be familiar as the term that the Greek philosopher Aristotle (384–322 BC) uses in his *Poetics* for the personal defect or frailty – the tragic flaw – that brings about the ruin of a prosperous or eminent man who is neither utterly villainous nor totally good, like, for instance, Oedipus. Hamartíā is a derivative of the verb hamartánein '(of a spear) to miss the mark, (in general) to fail in one's purpose, fall short, go wrong.'"

Surprisingly, both *chet* and *hamartia* are defined as misses the mark. Maimonides and Aristotle agreed.

Chapter Thirty-Six
The Mysterious Origin of the Passover Haroset

Many Jewish practices are not as old as people think and had no religious significance when first introduced. We do not even know how or when most Jewish practices began and why. We can only guess. In many instances our guesses reveal that lay people, even non-religious people, and in some instances, superstitious people started the practice, not Rabbis. The use of the sweet haroset at the Passover Seder table is a good example of some of this.

HISTORY OF HAROSET

in her easy to read, *Haroset: A Taste of Jewish History*, Dr. Susan Weingarten, a food historian, traces the development of the ancient haroset dish from its obscure origin sometime around the beginning of the Common Era. She offers readers "An intriguing exploration of one of the most mysterious symbolic Passover foods." She gives us the views of many rabbis and scholars, rationalists and mystics. Although unstated, it appears to me that we need to decide for ourselves what the haroset means for us, but she gives us a wealth of information to help us decide.

THE NAME

We do not know what the word haroset means, nor its application to food, and what it implies. Weingarten does not define the term. The word, found in Exodus 31:5 (twice), Exodus 35:33 (twice), with the root *ch-r-sh* in Isaiah 40:20, and Rashi to 31:5 defines it as "skilled work."[1] It is the name of a place in Judges 4:2, 13, and 16. The root means craftsman, plough, devise, discover, be silent, and a grove. Haroset in Modern Hebrew means industry and manufacture, and a *beit haroset* is a factory plant. None of this aids us in understanding the meaning of haroset as a food.[2]

THE INGREDIENTS OF HAROSET

While almost all haroset today is sweet, Maimonides (1138–1204) was the first to suggest the ingredients of haroset, and his view was that it should be acidic in memory of the harshness of the Israelites being required to build with clay.[3] Nevertheless, "The ingredients, and hence the taste, have varied over time."[4]

WHEN DID THE PRACTICE OF EATING HAROSET BEGIN?

The practice of eating haroset is not in the Bible, and we are doubtful of its use during the biblical period. Weingarten identifies the first mention of haroset in Mishnah *Pesachim* 10:5 and a similar passage in Tosephta *Pesachim* 10:9. The Mishnah, edited around 200 CE, states that unleavened bread, lettuce (which was very bitter in ancient times and was used as the *maror* [bitter herb]), and haroset were brought to the leader of the Seder "even though haroset is not a religious obligation [mitzvah]. R. Elazar ben Tzadok says, 'It is a religious obligation.'" The Mishnah gives us little information. It does not tell readers what the haroset is, when the practice arose to use it, its purpose, what were its ingredients, nor does it explain what Rabbi Elazar meant by, "It is a religious obligation." Was this statement a disagreement with the colleague who made the former statement? Or, was he saying that while it is not a biblical command, it is a significant part of the Seder?[5]

---

1. Israel Drazin, *Onkelos on the Torah: Exodus* (Jerusalem: Gefen Publishing House, 2006), 215.
2. The medieval Talmud commentators Rokeach and Mordekhai contend that haroset comes from *harsit*, a pale-colored earth that made pottery (Babylonian Talmud *Shabbat* 11b) because haroset reminds the Seder participants of the clay that the Egyptians forced the Israelites to use.
3. Rashi (1040–1105) also said the haroset should be acidic.
4. Curiously, some rabbis placed ground or scraped potsherds into haroset in the quest for authenticity, a reminder of the clay.
5. Maimonides wrote in *Mishneh Torah, Hilkhot Hametz U'Matzah*, 7:11, that it is only a lesser religious obligation.

While the foregoing seems to imply that haroset had a religious significance from the time of its introduction, it is possible that since the Bible required the eating of bitter herbs, the original haroset was simply a sweet sauce used to mollify the bitterness.

WHAT DOES THE HAROSET SIGNIFY?

The rabbis give many suggestions as to the significance of haroset.

1. "It must be thick in memory of the clay" that the Egyptians forced the Israelites to use to build cities or storehouses for them. Abbaye, commenting upon this explanation, said in *Pesachim* 116a, "Therefore you have to make acidic."
2. Jacob ben Asher (1269–1343) and others "It must be soft [or runny] in memory of blood." It is unclear what blood this recalls: blood of the Pascal lamb to mark their houses as a protection against having their first-born sons killed as were the Egyptian first-born sons or the first of the ten plagues when water turned to blood.
3. The Vilna Gaon suggested that haroset alludes to the manna that fell from heaven throughout the forty years that the Israelites wandered in the desert. He insisted therefore that haroset must be sweet.
4. In *Pesachim* 116a Rabbi Levi suggests that haroset contains apples as in Song of Songs 8:5, "I roused you under the apple tree." It is "In memory of the apple" which he and others interpreted as referring to God saving Israelite mothers who delivered children under apple trees to hide them from Egyptian officials when Pharaoh ordered to kill all male Israelite newborn children. Since ancient apples were sour, this view held that haroset was acidic.
5. There were also mystic notions such as the view of Rabbi Nachman of Breslov who suggested that the Hebrew letters of haroset can be rearranged into two new words, *has* and *rt*. The first meaning "mercy" and the second being the Hebrew name Ruth, the ancestor of King David, who in turn, is the ancestor of the messiah. Thus, haroset is a symbol of the future merciful messianic age.
6. Another mystic interpretation was made by Rabbi Isaac Luria (1534–1572) who when arranging letters saw the word haroset referring to the building of the ancient Tabernacle used during the time of Moses in the desert, "the earthly home of the Shekhinah, the seat of the Divine Presence."

In short, it appears that the introduction of haroset into the Seder, and other Seder practices, were to remind the Seder participants of the Egyptian experience of their ancestors and/or the mercy of God who delivered them.

WHAT WAS THE ORIGIN OF THE SEDER AND THE HAROSET?

The consensus among scholars is that the Seder is a copy of the Greek/Roman symposium meal and it is therefore reasonable to assume that haroset is a copy of one of the activities during the symposium. The rabbis used the symposium model to prompt Jews to recall the Egyptian slavery, the divine rescue to freedom, and the need for all Jews to feel as if they are enslaved and work toward creating a civilization where all people, not only Jews, can live in peace and safety, and be happy. For the basic Torah command is "Love thy neighbor as thyself."

While the symposium was the basic model, all the elements of it were changed. The term Seder means "order." It is the order arranged to use practices to move toward this goal. For instance, Jews learned that they should do as the Greeks and Romans in the symposium. This meant leaning during the meal to signify that they are free people, at leisure, and work to help others have this leisure as well. While the Greeks and Romans spoke about philosophy at their symposiums, as in Plato's famed book on philosophy called *Symposium*, Jews were encouraged to speak about the enslavement and freedom, and were told that speaking more on these subjects would earn them "praise." Wine was drunk at the symposiums, glass after glass, but the rabbis limited the drinking to four cups not just to limit inebriation, but to recall the four expressions used in the Torah to describe God's deliverance of the Israelite slaves. The passing of a ladle went around for hand washing. Appetizers such as lettuce and eggs introduced the meal, including the dipping of some foods into sauces. The Jews did so as well, but the dipping was into salt water to recall the tears of the enslaved ancestors, and into haroset in which rabbis explained the differences about what they symbolized.

WHY IS THE PREPARATION OF THE HAROSET USUALLY A MALE TASK?

Weingarten explains that the practice is sexist, "if haroset is really a mitzvah then it becomes important, and therefore something not beneath a man's dignity to prepare, even something too important to leave to 'mere' women. One modern rabbinic text I read even says that simply laying out the Seder table may be too important to be left to women."[6]

SUMMARY

In short, haroset is far from what most people thought it is. We have no idea when or why it started, but it seems clear that it was connected in post-biblical times to Greek and Roman culture, although it was clearly reinterpreted and given the meaning the Bible wanted, which was to recall, the slavery and the exodus. Does it recall the clay and the bricks that burdened the Israelite slaves? Or, does it remind users of divine love, as commentators saw God helping Israelite women under apple trees? Rabbis differ. Perhaps we should decide to see all the significances in this mysterious substance.

6. She identifies the source as M.Y. Weingarten, *HaSeder HaAruch: Kol Bo L'Seder Leil Pesach* (Jerusalem, 1993), 108–9, and is quick to add that the man is not her relative.

Chapter Thirty-Seven
Who Are the Most Influential Jews of All Time?

There is a known listing of influential Jews, which Michael Shapiro has combined in 387 pages in his 1995 book, *The Jewish 100: A Ranking of the Most Influential Jews of All Time*. We may or may not agree with his selections, but who are the Jews who influenced our lives, how, and are we living up to that inspiration?

SHAPIRO'S LIST

The list and biographies of the listees is interesting in what it includes and excludes. The list also discusses people that would surprise us. The following are some examples. (1) People who do not identify themselves as Jewish, such as Gustav Mahler who converted to Christianity. (2) People we never suspected were Jewish, like Marcel Proust. (3) People we may think were not heroic like Queen Esther. (4) The impact of those least suspected as having influenced us, such as the mystic Isaac Luria. Shapiro also left out men and women who many of us think did have a profound impact upon our lives.

Not surprisingly, for me the most influential Jew was Maimonides and the way he introduced me to a rational approach to life. I would place him on the top of the list with Moses. Shapiro has Maimonides as number 16 after Judas Iscariot and Gustav Mahler, two men who have no significant impact on my life. I recognize that Iscariot, according to the New Testament, pointed out Jesus to the Romans who then crucified him. Moreover, although I like Mahler's music, I do not like his songs, nor his decision to convert to Christianity to get a job, and I especially abhor his mistreatment of his wife.

NAMES I WOULD ADD

Another of my heroes is Arnold Ehrlich (1848–1919), known for having total recall and speaking 39 languages. Many of his views in his book, *Mikra Ki-Pheshuto, The Bible According to its Literal Meaning,* find their way into many of the books that I have written on the Bible, which is a subject that deeply interests me. Whether or not I agree with his views, they always make me think, and I include them to prompt others to think.

Rabbi Shmuel ben Meir, known as Rashbam (around 1085–1158), the grandson of Rashi is also a favorite character of mine. Like Maimonides and Ehrlich, he takes a rational approach to the Bible in reading what the Bible actually says rather than what Midrashim imagine the Bible is saying. Shapiro includes Rashi as number 20, and does not mention Rashbam. Children learn the Bible together with Rashi's midrashic views, and elementary Jewish schools do not mention Rashbam, which is unfortunate. He criticized his grandfather's methodology, even to his face, and Rashbam reports that Rashi often agreed with him to the point that if he had the chance to do it over, he would have followed Rashbam's methodology of explaining what the text states and not inventive inspirational notions.[1]

---

1. As I footnoted in my *Mysteries of Judaism I*.

Rashi's grandson, Rashbam, who wrote a generally rational Bible commentary, criticized his grandfather harshly for inserting midrashic explanations into his commentary and not sticking to the plain meaning of the biblical passages. In his commentary on Genesis 37:1, he told his readers that he upbraided his grandfather for the way he explained the Torah, and that Rashi assured him that he agreed with him. Rashi told him that if he had years to write new explanations, he would write a book in the way that Rashbam wrote his commentary.

In Genesis 49:17, where Rashi states that the verse is referring to the judge Samson, who would not be born for another couple of centuries, Rashbam angrily writes that anyone who thinks that this passage is speaking about Samson doesn't know how to understand the Torah.

In Deuteronomy 15:18, Scripture mandates that slave owners must give their Hebrew slaves gifts when they set them free. The Torah continues: "It should not seem hard to you . . . because he gave you double the service of a hired man." Rashi (based on Midrash *Sifrei*) proposes that Scripture's "double" means that Hebrew slaves work day and night, while hired employees works only during the day; the nighttime work is when the master gives the slave a Canaanite slave so that he can have children from the union that would belong to him as slaves. Rashbam calls this interpretation "foolish" and "vapor." The plain meaning of the verse, he says, is that

A good example of Rashbam's technique is his revelation that according to the Bible, the day begins in the morning, not at night. For in Genesis 1, the Bible speaks of divine creations during each of six days, then states that this was followed by "and there was evening and there was morning, one day [a second day, etc.]." These verses clearly state that the day ends and begins again when the sun rises.[2]

I would have also included Rabbi Akiva and Rabbi Ishmael, both of whom lived in the second century CE. Neither one is on Shapiro's list. They had different ideas on how to interpret the Bible. Rabbi Akiva who the Romans butchered around 135 CE is an important influential teacher because his view and not that of Rabbi Ishmael, who apparently escaped, became the accepted view. Rabbi Akiva's view influenced the teachings of Midrashim, Rashi, and most Bible commentators. They are the basis of virtually all sermons that congregants hear from rabbis today in synagogues. These are not the views of Maimonides, Rashbam, and Ehrlich, which I think is a shame. I also think that congregants should recognize the basis for the sermons and interpretations they are hearing so that they can evaluate whether they feel it is a correct explanation of the biblical verse. The lesson in most instances is correct, but contrary to the rabbi, the lesson is not in the Bible but based upon a midrashic lesson.[3]

Rabbi Akiva insisted that since God dictated the Torah to Moses, letter by letter, and since God is all-wise, God will say exactly what is intended, with no superfluous letter. Therefore, every letter of the Torah text is meaningful in discovering teachings that are not explicit in the Torah text. In contrast, Rabbi Ishmael insisted that we read Torah as we read other books because "the Torah speaks in human language." Repetitions that abound in the Torah do not imply a new lesson

---

the "master" should not feel bad in having paid for slaves twice, once when he purchased slaves and now again when he must also give the slaves gifts.

The eleventh-century rationalist Abraham ibn Ezra, who lived around the same time, wrote mockingly about Rashi that he translates the Torah according to its plain meaning and he is correct – one time out of a thousand.

2. Also, in the temple the sacrifices began in the morning.

3. Maimonides pointed this out in his extended essay called *Chelek*. Those who think that Midrashim are true are fools. So too are those who dismiss Midrashim entirely since they are untrue. Midrashim are important even though the method used to derive the message is false because the message in most cases is true.

or new halakha. As in human literature, repetitions in the Torah may simply be emphasizing that which is already stated, and not adding something new.

OTHERS THAT I WOULD HAVE INCLUDED

According to Jewish law, a man or woman is a Jew if his or her mother was Jewish. This includes the descendant of a female ancestress whose daughter was automatically Jewish, whose daughter of the third generation was automatically Jewish, and so on. Thus, even after many generations, a child, male or female, descending from a line of women whose ancestor was Jewish is Jewish according to Jewish law.

Accordingly, one could include people like Elvis Presley.[4] It would also include President Lyndon B. Johnson who was Jewish because his grandmother and mother were Jewish and Judaism passes down generation to generation from the mother. Because his granddaughter was the child of a non-Jewish woman, she converted to Judaism.[5]

IN SHORT

I suggest that everyone should have their own list of the people who influenced them the most. They should ask themselves why they chose the person for the list, and decide if the individual still influences them and why.

---

4. Jerry Klinger, President of the Jewish American Society for Historic Preservation, wrote about him in many places.
5. Dov Peretz Elkins, *Four Rabbis at Lunch* (New York: Ktav Publishing House, 2019).

Chapter Thirty-Eight
The World Is Filled with Jews

Most people are convinced that there are comparatively few Jews in the world. In 2001, there were roughly 13.3 million, about 1.4 percent of the world population of which 4.9 million lived in Israel, and 8.3 million outside the Holy Land. Logic would dictate that the actual figure is many times that number and percentage. It is even possible that Jews outnumber the number of all other western religions.

A RADICAL VIEW ABOUT JEWS

First, let us look at the most radical view of the number of Jews.

The twelfth century Spanish poet Yehuda Halevi was a well-respected man in his lifetime. Today he is known for his poetical defense of Judaism called the *Kuzari*, a book that is admired by so many Jews that numerous rabbis give classes and lectures on it, as if it is a holy book. Unfortunately, neither these rabbis nor their congregants delve deeply enough into the volume to understand it, as Hillel Halkin does.[1]

After analyzing Halevi's views, Halkin compares Halevi's *Kuzari* to Maimonides's rational *Guide of the Perplexed.* "The reader attracted to Maimonides will find the *Kuzari* irrational in its assumptions, careless in its logic, dismissive of scientific thinking, presumptuously ethnocentric."

I agree with Hillel Halkin. I especially disagree with four of Halevi's key points.

1. Hillel Halkin, *Yehuda Halevi* (New York: Nextbook Schocken, 2010).

JEWS ARE BIOLOGICALLY SUPERIOR TO ALL OTHER PEOPLE

Halevi teaches that Jews are biologically superior to all other people. Non-Jews are somewhere between animals and Jews. Even converts to Judaism are unable to reach the level of Jews because they lack their biology. They remain in the lower class. I dislike this notion, and think that God created and loves all people, and we should respect everyone. Furthermore, there were countless non-Jews converting to Judaism and marrying Jews throughout the centuries. These included many important biblical figures such as Moses's wife Zipporah and King David's ancestress Ruth. Those who believe the future messiah will descend from David will have to agree that the messiah descended from a convert. Using Halevi's logic, the number of Jews today is approximately zero.

THERE IS PROOF THAT JUDAISM IS THE CORRECT RELIGION

Second, I also do not think that his proof that Judaism is correct is logical. He argues as fact that the Sinai revelation occurred because millions of people who saw it passed on what they saw to the next generation. Thus, according to Halevi, we have reliable witness reports. I am not questioning revelation, just his logic. We know that incorrect ideas pass from generation to generation. We also know that other religions make the same unreliable claim.

MOSES'S GENERATION WERE ALL PROPHETS

Third, he states that all the Israelites who left Egypt were prophets. Anyone reading the plain words of the Torah will see that many of the Israelites were rabble. This is a clearly stated in the description of their behavior and by the words of Moses and of God.

JEWS ARE GOD'S CHOSEN PEOPLE

He insisted that Jews are the only people that God loves; God gives Jews special attention and even unearned assistance. Only Jews receive prophecy, which is a unique and valuable gift from God, expressing God's love for the Jews. Jews are smarter and more virtuous; they, and only they, with perhaps a few exceptions are granted life after death. In his *Kuzari* 1:27, he writes: "Any gentile who joins us [as a proselyte] unconditionally shares our good fortune, without, however, being quite equal to us."

Thus, to illustrate Halevi's view of non-Jewish converts to Judaism: one cannot convert a camel into a sheep by a conversion process of immersion and circumcision. The result is a clean and circumcised camel, but it is not a sheep.

THE BIBLICAL VIEW

The Bible seems to confirm Halevi's position that Jews are chosen by God for special loving treatment. Deuteronomy 7:6, for example, assures the Jew that, "you are a people consecrated to the Lord your God: of all the people on earth the Lord your God chose you to be His treasured people." Deuteronomy 7:7–8 reports God stating that He chose the Israelites "because the Lord loved you."

Yet, appearances are deceiving. First, while it is true that God chose and loves the Israelites, He chose/created, and loves all creations. The prophet Amos teaches this important lesson. In 9:7, he quotes God as saying that God loves and gives special attention to all nations: "Are you not like the children of the Ethiopians to Me, children of Israel? Have I not brought up Israel out of the land of Egypt, and the Philistines from Caphtor, and Aram from Kir?" All nations are chosen and have a divine mission and responsibility.

Second, this idea of God showing love to a people, whether Jew or non-Jew, is contingent upon the people obeying the law. It is part of a reciprocal covenantal relationship.

The love and caring assurances God makes to people is similar to husbands and wives saying to each other, "I love you." These expressions of love do not require the spouse who is speaking to add, "on the condition that you act properly to me." One understands this reciprocal love. A one-sided relationship cannot exist. The relationship falls apart when one party neglects the other.

This anti-Halevi understanding of God choosing people for a reciprocal relationship teaches that no human being should sit back passively and arrogantly bask in the love of God. Nor should they act like Hitler and consider people unlike them as *Untermenschen*. People have a responsibility in this God-human relationship to act in a positive loving manner to all that God created.

A STATEMENT IN THE TALMUD

Second-century rabbis identify single scriptural commands that they feel show the essence of Judaism. Rabbi Akiva suggests, "Love thy neighbor as thyself." Simeon ben Zoma, also encouraging respect for all humanity and emphasizing that a people is not chosen over another, states that the fundamental teaching of the Torah is at the outset of the Torah: God created *all people* in the divine image.

THE VIEW OF MAIMONIDES

Ben Zoma's teaching is also the teaching of Maimonides who bases his entire philosophy on his recognition that all humans are divinely created creatures and inherently the same. He begins his philosophical work *Guide of the Perplexed,* in chapter 1, by telling his readers, as did ben Zoma, that the Bible instructs us that humans, not only Jews, were created in the *tzelem Elohim* (the image of God) (*Genesis* 1:27); all were created in God's image with the potential to develop themselves.

MY VIEW ABOUT THE NUMBER OF JEWS IS BASED ON WELL-RECOGNIZED FACTS

We know of the persecution of Jews for generations and the abandonment of Judaism in many ways. Thousands underwent forced conversions. Myriad of others converted to secure an education or a job or to avoid harassment. Thousands did not convert but hid the fact that they were Jews and acted as non-Jews. The original Jews who did this retained their Jewishness, but their children and grandchildren did not. They simply continued to be non-Jews as their parents acted, but like it or not, they were descendants of Jews, they had "Jewish blood." Thousands of Jewish women suffered the abusiveness of rape during pogroms and attacks beginning with the first crusaders in 1095 who made their way across Europe to secure the Holy Land from the Arabs. The intermarriage rate between Jews and non-Jews has always been high. Ezra and Nehemiah railed against it separately and on more than a single occasion unsuccessfully in biblical days. Today, it is as high as 58 percent. Their children may choose to live as non-Jews, but they too carry Jewish blood. The daughters of two recent presidents, Clinton and Trump, married Jewish husbands but only Ivanka Trump converted. While Chelsea Clinton did not convert and her children are not considered Jewish by Jewish law which calls people Jewish only if they are descendants of a Jewish mother or convert, her children, like it or not, also have "Jewish blood."

Even Adolph Hitler may have had a Jewish ancestor. There are those who believe that his grandmother was a household cook to a Jewish family and had a son with a 19-year-old son of the family who became Hitler's grandfather. Even the grandchildren of Haman may have converted according to the Talmud, and learned and taught Torah in Bnei Brak in Israel.[2] Jews had to leave Spain from 1492 until 1950. Those remaining converted and married others and passed on the Jewish blood in Spain and elsewhere. Some of Christopher Columbus's crew, including the first European to set foot on the new land, and perhaps even Columbus himself, were Jews forcibly converted to Christianity.[3] It is possible that along with President Lyndon B. Johnson, President Abraham Lincoln also descended from Jews.[4]

Even if these claims of Jewish ancestry are untrue, what is clearly true is that Jews had multiple sexual relationships with non-Jews, produced children, who in turn gave birth to more children, with the result that there are more Jews than people think.

If we use the metaphor "Jewish blood," we can say that the descendants of these people had Jewish blood. We can also say that the copious relationships between Jewish and non-Jewish people were so numerous and as such resulted in multiple births that it is even possible that there may be only a few living people in western countries today that lack Jewish blood.

Perhaps this understanding of the connection of Jews and non-Jews can spur better relationships between the religions.

---

2. Babylonian Talmud, *Gittin* 57b, *Sanhedrin* 69b and 96b. Chatam Sofer also contends in his commentary to the biblical book Esther that Haman was Mordecai's slave before he rose to prominence and Mordecai had converted him to Judaism.

3. Cecil Roth, *A History of the Jews From Earliest Times through the Six Day War* (NY: Schocken Books, 1970); Deborah R. Prinz, *On the Chocolate Trial* (Woodstock, VT: Jewish Lights Publishing, 2012).

4. David Max Eichhorn, *Joys of Jewish Folklore: A Journey from New Amsterdam to Beverly Hills and Beyond* (New York: Jonathan David Publications, 1981). This book has many fascinating tales, including: In 1916 nuns were being sanctified as wives of Jesus. Two rabbis were in the crowed. When asked why they were present, they replied, we are related to the groom.

Afterword

Most people, Jews and non-Jews have wrong ideas about Judaism. They read the Bible but see only what they want or need to see, but not what the Bible actually says. It is as if they are looking into a mirror, not the Bible. Many of these wrong ideas are those they learnt as children; fit to entertain children, but not helping people improve themselves, and to become better people. These wrong ideas affect their lives.

We saw that there are multiple misconceptions about what the Bible states about creation, the patriarchs, the children of the patriarchs, and much more. Below are some of the 100 or so items addressed:

- The Bible's fundamental teaching is not what many think.
- Why did it take God six days to create the world?
- There are multiple questions raised by the Adam and Eve stories, including: Are there two versions about the creation of Eve? Did other people exist before or during the lifetime of Adam and Eve and their children? Where did Cain, Abel, and Seth get their wives?
- Should Jews accept the concept of original sin? Is it in the Torah?
- Why does the Torah say it was a talking snake that enticed Eve? Why did the snake do so? Was sex involved? Is the story a parable?
- What can we know about God?
- *Y-H-V-H* and *Elohim* as well as other so-called names of God are not God's names.
- How can we say that the revelation of the Torah was at Sinai when it describes events that occurred after the Israelites left Sinai?
- Should we accept the finding of Abraham ibn Ezra, Spinoza, and others that Moses could not have composed everything in the Torah, the primary example, recognized by the Talmud, is the tale of Moses's death and burial?

- Should we agree that there are many indications that the biblical figures after the time of Moses until around 620 BCE and maybe later, including prophets and leaders of the people, knew nothing about the Torah and repeatedly violated Torah commands?
- Did Jacob wrestle with an angel and did Balaam speak with his donkey?
- Why does the Bible devote so much space to sacrifices?
- The Bible does not identify Jerusalem as a holy city or suggest that it is the only place to have sacrifices. In fact, there were sacrifices in Shiloh, where the prophet Samuel lived, for 369 years beginning not very long after the Israelites entered Canaan.
- Relying on God for help can result in tragedy.
- We do not know how or when most Jewish practices began and why they began.
- Reciting the Shema on one's deathbed originated from two legends, both misunderstood, a practice that began around 1800.
- The Torah does not tell us everything and leaves much to the reader to imagine.
- Often a repetition seems to conflict with the prior description in a significant manner.
- Differences in spelling occurs frequently, as in the two versions of the Decalogue.
- We can only guess about the meaning of many biblical words.
- Christians were the first to divide the Torah into chapters, which Jews accepted even though it is sometimes not rational.
- Rabbis differ on whether the Torah is a divine language with God saying exactly what God wants said. This is the view of Rabbi Akiva, Rashi, many others, and most synagogue sermons. The view of Rabbi Ishmael, Maimonides, ibn Ezra, and others is that the Torah speaks in human language with repetitions not teaching new lessons, but only repeated for emphasis or a similar reason.
- Scripture frequently, yet briefly describes an event leaving out details, which it later adds when the event repeats.
- Both rabbis and scholars differ among themselves on whether certain biblical stories or events are actually historical, or a dream, or parable.

Sources

Altschuler, David. *Metzudot David.*

Avigad, Nahman and Yigal Yadin. *A Genesis Apocryphon: A Scroll from the Wilderness of Judaea.* Jerusalem: Magnes Press, Hebrew University, 1956.

Babylonian Talmud tractates: *Avodah Zara, Bava Batra, Berakhot, Chagigah, Gittin, Ketubot, Makkot, Menachot, Nedarim, Rosh Hashanah, Sanhedrin, Shabbat, Ta'anit, Sotah, Yoma, Zevachim.*

Bar Eitan, Zev. *Abravanel's World of Torah: Bereshit.* Renaissance Torah Press, 2012.

Bass, Shabbetai ben Joseph. *Siftei Chachamim.*

Ben Asher, Jacob. *Tur.*

ben Meshulam Yerucham, Rabbi. *Sefer Toldot Adam v'Chava.*

ben Nachman, Moses (Nachmanides). *Disputation at Barcelona: Ramban.* Translated by Charles B. Chavel. BNB Publishing, 2017.

———, *Ramban Commentary on the Torah.* Translated by Charles B. Chavel. New York: Judaica Press, 2005.

———, *Hasagot on Sefer Ha-Mitzvoth of Ramban, Mitzvot Aseh*

———, "Torat Hashem Temimah." In *Kitvei Ha-Ramban,* edited by Charles Ber Chavel: Jerusalem: Mossad Harav Kook, 1963.

Da'at Zekeinim Miba'alei Hatosafot.

Danzig, Avraham, Rabbi. *Chochmat Adam.*

Davidson, Herbert A. *Maimonides the Rationalist.* The Littman Library of Jewish Civilization, 2011.

de León, Moses. *Zohar.*

Diamond, James Arthur, Menachem Kellner, and Seth Kadish. *Reinventing Maimonides in Contemporary Jewish Thought.* The Littman Library of Jewish Civilization, Liverpool, 2019.

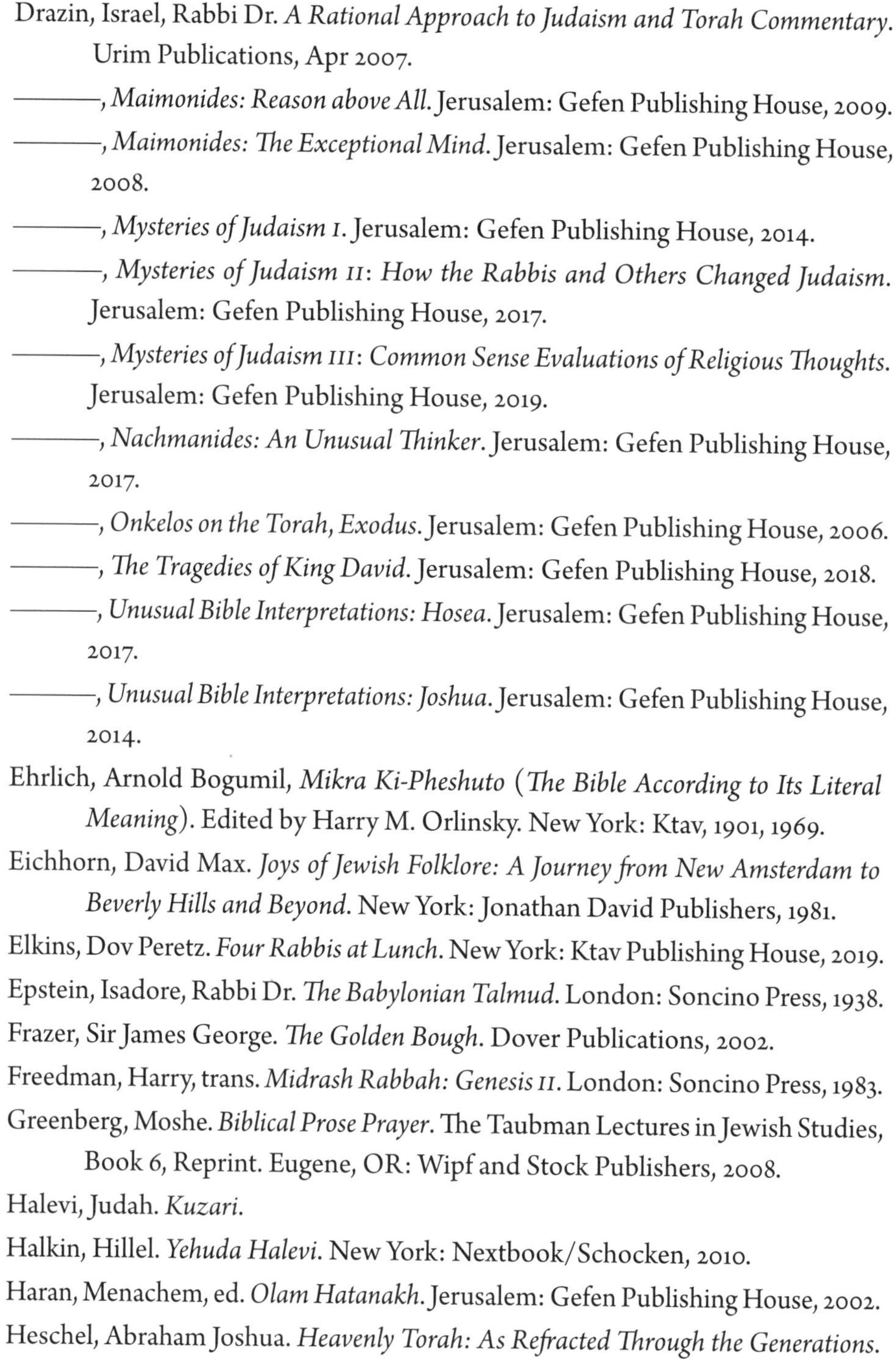

Drazin, Israel, Rabbi Dr. *A Rational Approach to Judaism and Torah Commentary.* Urim Publications, Apr 2007.

———, *Maimonides: Reason above All.* Jerusalem: Gefen Publishing House, 2009.

———, *Maimonides: The Exceptional Mind.* Jerusalem: Gefen Publishing House, 2008.

———, *Mysteries of Judaism I.* Jerusalem: Gefen Publishing House, 2014.

———, *Mysteries of Judaism II: How the Rabbis and Others Changed Judaism.* Jerusalem: Gefen Publishing House, 2017.

———, *Mysteries of Judaism III: Common Sense Evaluations of Religious Thoughts.* Jerusalem: Gefen Publishing House, 2019.

———, *Nachmanides: An Unusual Thinker.* Jerusalem: Gefen Publishing House, 2017.

———, *Onkelos on the Torah, Exodus.* Jerusalem: Gefen Publishing House, 2006.

———, *The Tragedies of King David.* Jerusalem: Gefen Publishing House, 2018.

———, *Unusual Bible Interpretations: Hosea.* Jerusalem: Gefen Publishing House, 2017.

———, *Unusual Bible Interpretations: Joshua.* Jerusalem: Gefen Publishing House, 2014.

Ehrlich, Arnold Bogumil, *Mikra Ki-Pheshuto* (*The Bible According to Its Literal Meaning*). Edited by Harry M. Orlinsky. New York: Ktav, 1901, 1969.

Eichhorn, David Max. *Joys of Jewish Folklore: A Journey from New Amsterdam to Beverly Hills and Beyond.* New York: Jonathan David Publishers, 1981.

Elkins, Dov Peretz. *Four Rabbis at Lunch.* New York: Ktav Publishing House, 2019.

Epstein, Isadore, Rabbi Dr. *The Babylonian Talmud.* London: Soncino Press, 1938.

Frazer, Sir James George. *The Golden Bough.* Dover Publications, 2002.

Freedman, Harry, trans. *Midrash Rabbah: Genesis II.* London: Soncino Press, 1983.

Greenberg, Moshe. *Biblical Prose Prayer.* The Taubman Lectures in Jewish Studies, Book 6, Reprint. Eugene, OR: Wipf and Stock Publishers, 2008.

Halevi, Judah. *Kuzari.*

Halkin, Hillel. *Yehuda Halevi.* New York: Nextbook/Schocken, 2010.

Haran, Menachem, ed. *Olam Hatanakh.* Jerusalem: Gefen Publishing House, 2002.

Heschel, Abraham Joshua. *Heavenly Torah: As Refracted Through the Generations.* Translated by Gordon Tucker. Continuum, 2006.

Heschel, Abraham Joshua. *Torah min Ha-Shamayim Be-Aspaḳlaryah shel Ha-Dorot.* New York: Defus Shontsin, 1962.

Hesiod, *Works and Days.* c. 700 BC.

Hoffman, Rabbi Evan. *Thoughts on the Parashah.* NY, New Rochelle: Congregation Anshe Sholom, August 17, 2019.

Horowitz, Isaiah, Rabbi. *Shney Luchot Habrit.* NY: Lambda Publishers Inc., 2000.

Irving, Washington, *Rip Van Winkle,* 1820.

Jerusalem Talmud: *Berakhot.*

Jewish Bible Quarterly. Jerusalem: Jewish Bible Association, 28:1, 2000.

Kamara, Peter. *Ancient Roman Mythology.* Book Sales: Ancient Mythology Series, 1997.

Karo, Joseph. *Shulchan Arukh*

Kellner, Menachem. *Maimonides on the "Decline of the Generations" and the Nature of Rabbinic Authority.* New York: SUNY Press, 1996.

Kiel, Yehuda, *Sefer Daat Mikra: Bereishit.* Jerusalem: Mossad Harav Kook, 1997.

Kohn, Maor, and Mati Cohen. *A Beginner's Guide to Skepticism.* Simple Story, 2019.

Kraemer, Joel L. *Perspectives on Maimonides.* The Littman Library of Jewish Civilization, 1996.

Maccoby, Hyam. *Judaism on Trial: Jewish-Christian Disputations in the Middle Ages.* The Littman Library of Jewish Civilization, 1993.

Maimonides, Moses (Rambam), *Commentary on the Aphorism of Hippocrates.* Maimonides Research Institute, 1987.

———, *Mishneh Torah* (Code of Law and Ethics), c.1170–1180 CE.

———, *Sefer Hamitzvot L'harambam im Hasagot Haramban (Book of Commandments).* Jerusalem: Mossad Harav Kook, 1981.

———, *The Guide of the Perplexed of Maimonides,* University of Chicago Press, 1974.

Marcus, Ivan G. "Performative Midrash in the Memory of Ashkenazi Martyrs." In *Midrash Unbound: Transformations and Innovations.* Oxford: Littman Library of Jewish Civilization, Liverpool University Press, 2013.

Marx, Karl. "A Contribution to the Critique of Hegel's Philosophy of Right." Deutsch-Franzosische Jahrbucher, 1844. https://www.marxists.org/archive/marx/works/1843/critique-hpr/intro.htm

Midrashim: *Deuteronomy Rabba, Genesis Rabba, Mekhilta d'Rabbi Ishmael, Sifrei.*

Mishnaot: *Pesachim, Zevachim, Yoma.*

Plato. *The Symposium.*

Polonsky, Pinchas. *Religious Zionism of Rav Kook.* CreateSpace, 2017.

Prinz, Deborah R. *On the Chocolate Trail.* Woodstock, VT: Jewish Lights Publishing, 2012.

Roth, Cecil. *A History of the Jews: From Earliest Times Through the Six Day War.* NY: Schocken Books, 1970.

Schnitzer, Cary, Dr. *Understanding Adam's Sin and its Rectification.* Independently published, 2019.

Schreiber, Moses (Chatam Sofer). *Ḥotam Ha-Melekh.* Brooklyn, NY: Dov HaKohen Fink, 2010.

Shapiro, Marc B. *Studies in Maimonides and His Interpreters.* PA, Scranton: University of Scranton Press, 2008.

Shapiro, Michael. *The Jewish 100: A Ranking of the Most Influential Jews of all Time.* Paumanok, 2012.

Shaw, George Bernard. *Caesar and Cleopatra.* Penguin Classics, 2006.

Sîn-lēqi-unninni, *Epic of Gilgamesh,* c. 1000 BC.

Soloveitchik, Rabbi Joseph B. *Days of Deliverance: Essays on Purim and Chanukah.* NY: KTAV Publishing House Inc., 2007.

Soloveitchik, Rabbi Joseph B. *The Koren Mesorat HaRav Siddur.* Jerusalem: Koren Publishers, 2011.

Sophocles. *Theban Plays: Oedipus Rex, Oedipus at Colonus, and Antigone,* 406 BCE.

Speiser, Ephraim Avigdor. *The Anchor Bible: Genesis,* Doubleday, 1964.

Targumim: *Onkelos.*

Tosephtot: *Pesachim.*

Twersky, Isadore. *Introduction to the Code of Maimonides.* New Haven, Conn.: Yale University Press, 1980.

Urbach, Ephraim E. *The Sages: Their Concepts and Beliefs.* Translated by Israel Abrahams. Cambridge, Mass: Harvard University Press 1987.

Weingarten, Moshe Yaakov, Rabbi. *HaSeder HaAruch: Kol Bo L'Seder Leil Pesach.* Jerusalem, 1993.

Weingarten, Susan, Dr. *Haroset: A Taste of Jewish History.* New Milford, CT: The Toby Press, 2019.

Wells, Herbert George. *When the Sleeper Wakes.* CreateSpace Independent Publishing, 2011.

Index

H

I

J

K

L

S

T

U

W

Y

Z

Biography of the Author

EDUCATION: Dr. Drazin, born in 1935, received three rabbinical degrees in 1957, a BA in Theology in 1957, an MEd in Psychology in 1966, a JD in Law in 1974, an MA in Hebrew Literature in 1978, and a PhD with honors in Aramaic Literature in 1981. Thereafter, he completed two years of post-graduate study in both Philosophy and Mysticism and graduated the US Army's Command and General Staff College and its War College for generals in 1985.

MILITARY: Brigadier General Drazin entered Army Active Duty, at age 21, as the youngest US Chaplain ever to serve on active duty. He served on active duty from 1957 to 1960 in Louisiana and Germany, and then joined the active reserves and soldiered, in increasing grades, with half a dozen units. From 1978 until 1981, he lectured at the US Army Chaplains School on legal subjects. In March 1981, the Army requested that he take leave from civil service and return to active duty to handle special constitutional issues. He was responsible for preparing the defense in the trial challenging the constitutionality of the Army Chaplaincy. The military chaplaincies of all the uniformed services, active and reserve, as well as the Veteran's Administration, were attacked utilizing a constitutional rationale and could have been disbanded. The Government won the action in 1984 and Drazin was awarded the prestigious Legion of Merit. Drazin returned to civilian life and the active reserves in 1984 as Assistant Chief of Chaplains, the highest reserve officer position available in the Army Chaplaincy with the rank of Brigadier General. He was the first Jewish person to serve in this capacity in the US Army. During his military career, he revolutionized the role of military chaplains making them officers responsible for the free exercise of rights of all military personnel; requiring them to provide for the needs of people of all faiths as well as atheists. General Drazin completed this four-year tour of duty with honors in March 1988, culminating a total of 31 years of military duty.

ATTORNEY: Israel Drazin graduated from law school in 1974 and immediately began a private practice. He handled virtually all manners of suits including domestic, criminal, bankruptcy, accident, and contract cases. He joined with his son in 1993 and formed offices in Columbia and Dundalk, Maryland. Dr. Drazin stopped actively practicing law in 1997, after 23 years.

CIVIL SERVICE: Israel Drazin joined the US Civil Service in 1962 after his active duty service and remained a civil service employee with occasional leave for military duty until retirement in 1990. Upon retirement, he accumulated 31 years of creditable service. During his US Civil Service career, he held many positions; including, being an Equal Opportunity Consultant in the 1960s (advising insurance company top executives regarding civil rights and equal employment) and the head of Medicare's Civil Litigation Staff (supervising a team of lawyers who handled suits filed by and against the government's Medicare program). He was the director handling all of Maryland's Federal Agencies' relationship with the United Fund.

RABBI: Dr. Drazin was ordained as a rabbi in 1957 at Ner Israel Rabbinical College in Baltimore, Maryland and subsequently received semichot from two other rabbis. He entered on Army active duty in 1957. He left active duty in 1960 and officiated as a weekend rabbi at several synagogues, including being the first rabbi in Columbia, Maryland. He continued the uninterrupted weekend rabbinical practice until 1974 and then officiated as a rabbi on an intermittent basis until 1987. His rabbinical career totaled 30 years.

PHILANTHROPY: Dr. Drazin served as the Executive Director of the Jim Joseph Foundation, a charitable foundation that gives money to support Jewish education, for just over four years from September 2000 to November 2004.

AUTHOR: Israel Drazin is the author of fifty-five books, some in the process of publishing, more than 500 popular and scholarly articles, and over 6,800 book, music and movie reviews that appear on Amazon and other sites. He wrote a book about the case he handled for the US Army, edited two books on legends by his father, children's books with his daughter, and many scholarly books on the philosopher Maimonides and on the Aramaic translation of the Bible. His website is www.booksnthoughts.com and he publishes two essays on this site every week as well as on the Times of Israel and the San Diego Jewish World.

LECTURES: Dr. Drazin delivered lectures at Howard Community College, Lynn University, and the US Army Chaplains School, and continues to give lectures to military chaplains.

MEMBERSHIPS AND AWARDS: Brigadier General Drazin received the prestigious Albert Nelson Marquis Lifetime Achievement Award in 2019. He can still practice law in Maryland, the Federal Court, and before the US Supreme Court. He is a member of several attorney Bar Associations and the Rabbinical Council of America. Drazin received many military awards, the RCA 1985 Joseph Hoenig Memorial Award, and the Jewish Welfare Board 1986 Distinguished Service Award. Mayor Kurt Schmoke, of Baltimore, Maryland, named February 8, 1988 "Israel Drazin Day." A leading Baltimore Synagogue named him "Man of the Year" in 1990. He is included in the recent editions of *Who's Who in World Jewry*, *Who's Who in American Law*, *Who's Who in Biblical Studies and Archaeology*, *Marquis Who's Who* of 2019, and other *Who's Who* volumes.